BEST-LOVED BAKING COLLECTION™

Ultimate CHOCOLATE RECIPES

America...
BRAND-NAME RECIPES®

Pictured on the front cover: Easy Double Chocolate Chip Brownies *(page 72).*

Pictured on the back cover *(left to right):* Chocolate Square with Nutty Caramel Sauce *(page 82)* and Nestlé® Toll House® Chocolate Chip Pie *(page 109).*

ISBN: 0-8487-2878-5

Library of Congress Control Number: 2004104488

Manufactured in China.

8 7 6 5 4 3 2 1

Microwave Cooking: Microwave ovens vary in wattage. Use the cooking times as guidelines and check for doneness before adding more time.

Preparation/Cooking Times: Preparation times are based on the approximate amount of time required to assemble the recipe before cooking, baking, chilling or serving. These times include preparation steps such as measuring, chopping and mixing. The fact that some preparations and cooking can be done simultaneously is taken into account. Preparation of optional ingredients and serving suggestions is not included.

Contents

irresistible cookies

dark chocolate dreams

16 ounces bittersweet chocolate candy bars or bittersweet
 chocolate chips
¼ cup (½ stick) butter
½ cup all-purpose flour
¾ teaspoon ground cinnamon
½ teaspoon baking powder
¼ teaspoon salt
1½ cups sugar
 3 eggs
 1 teaspoon vanilla
 1 package (12 ounces) white chocolate chips
 1 cup chopped pecans, lightly toasted

1. Preheat oven to 350°F. Grease cookie sheets.

2. Coarsely chop chocolate bars; place in microwavable bowl. Add butter. Microwave at HIGH 2 minutes; stir. Microwave 1 to 2 minutes, stirring after 1 minute, or until chocolate is melted. Cool to lukewarm.

3. Combine flour, cinnamon, baking powder and salt in small bowl; set aside.

4. Beat sugar, eggs and vanilla at medium-high speed of electric mixer until very thick and mixture turns pale, about 6 minutes.

5. Reduce speed to low; slowly beat in chocolate mixture until well blended. Gradually beat in flour mixture until blended. Fold in white chocolate chips and pecans.

6. Drop dough by level ⅓ cupfuls onto prepared cookie sheets, spacing 3 inches apart. Place piece of plastic wrap over dough; flatten dough with fingertips to form 4-inch circles. Remove plastic wrap.

7. Bake 12 minutes or until just firm to the touch and surface begins to crack. *Do not overbake.* Cool cookies 2 minutes on cookie sheets; transfer to wire racks. Cool completely.

Makes 10 to 12 (5-inch) cookies

note: Cookies may be baked on ungreased cookie sheets lined with parchment paper. Cool cookies 2 minutes on cookie sheets; slide parchment paper and cookies onto countertop. Cool completely.

double chocolate walnut drops

$^3/_4$ cup (1$^1/_2$ sticks) butter or margarine, softened
$^3/_4$ cup granulated sugar
$^3/_4$ cup firmly packed light brown sugar
1 large egg
1 teaspoon vanilla extract
2$^1/_4$ cups all-purpose flour
$^1/_3$ cup unsweetened cocoa powder
1 teaspoon baking soda
$^1/_2$ teaspoon salt
1$^3/_4$ cups "M&M's"® Chocolate Mini Baking Bits
1 cup coarsely chopped English or black walnuts

Preheat oven to 350°F. Lightly grease cookie sheets; set aside. In large bowl cream butter and sugars until light and fluffy; beat in egg and vanilla. In medium bowl combine flour, cocoa powder, baking soda and salt; add to creamed mixture. Stir in "M&M's"® Chocolate Mini Baking Bits and nuts. Drop by heaping tablespoonfuls about 2 inches apart onto prepared cookie sheets. Bake 12 to 14 minutes for chewy cookies or 14 to 16 minutes for crispy cookies. Cool completely on wire racks. Store in tightly covered container.

Makes about 4 dozen cookies

variation: Shape dough into 2-inch-thick roll. Cover with plastic wrap; refrigerate. When ready to bake, slice dough into $^1/_4$-inch-thick slices and bake as directed.

white chocolate chunk & macadamia nut brownie cookies

1½ cups firmly packed light brown sugar
⅔ CRISCO® Stick or ⅔ cup CRISCO® all-vegetable shortening
1 tablespoon water
1 teaspoon vanilla
2 eggs
1½ cups all-purpose flour
⅓ cup unsweetened cocoa powder
½ teaspoon salt
¼ teaspoon baking soda
1 cup white chocolate chunks or chips
1 cup coarsely chopped macadamia nuts

1. Heat oven to 375°F. Place sheets of foil on countertop for cooling cookies.

2. Place brown sugar, ⅔ cup shortening, water and vanilla in large bowl. Beat at medium speed of electric mixer until well blended. Add eggs; beat well.

3. Combine flour, cocoa, salt and baking soda. Add to shortening mixture; beat at low speed just until blended. Stir in white chocolate chunks and macadamia nuts.

4. Drop dough by rounded measuring tablespoonfuls 2 inches apart onto ungreased baking sheet.

5. Bake one baking sheet at a time at 375°F for 7 to 9 minutes or until cookies are set. *Do not overbake.* Cool 2 minutes on baking sheet. Remove cookies to foil to cool completely.

Makes about 3 dozen cookies

double chocolate oat cookies →

 2 cups (12 ounces) semisweet chocolate pieces, divided
$^{1}/_{2}$ cup (1 stick) margarine or butter, softened
$^{1}/_{2}$ cup granulated sugar
 1 egg
$^{1}/_{4}$ teaspoon vanilla
$^{3}/_{4}$ cup all-purpose flour
$^{3}/_{4}$ cup QUAKER® Oats (quick or old fashioned, uncooked)
 1 teaspoon baking powder
$^{1}/_{4}$ teaspoon baking soda
$^{1}/_{4}$ teaspoon salt (optional)

Preheat oven to 375°F. Melt 1 cup chocolate pieces in small saucepan; set aside. Beat margarine and sugar until fluffy; add melted chocolate, egg and vanilla. Add combined flour, oats, baking powder, baking soda and salt; mix well. Stir in remaining chocolate pieces. Drop by rounded tablespoonfuls onto *ungreased* cookie sheets. Bake 8 to 10 minutes. Cool 1 minute on cookie sheets; remove to wire racks.

Makes about 3 dozen cookies

simpler than sin peanut chocolate cookies

 1 cup PETER PAN® Extra Crunchy Peanut Butter
 1 cup sugar
 1 egg, at room temperature and beaten
 2 teaspoons vanilla
 1 (6-ounce) dark or milk chocolate candy bar, broken into squares

Preheat oven to 350°F. In medium bowl, combine Peter Pan® Peanut Butter, sugar, egg and vanilla; mix well. Roll dough into 1-inch balls. Place 2 inches apart on ungreased cookie sheet. Bake 12 minutes. Remove from oven and place chocolate square in center of each cookie. Bake an additional 5 to 7 minutes or until cookies are lightly golden around edges. Cool 5 minutes. Remove to wire rack. Cool.

Makes 21 to 24 cookies

note: This simple recipe is unusual because it doesn't contain any flour—but it still makes great cookies!

chocolate x and o cookies

²/₃ cup butter or margarine, softened
1 cup sugar
2 teaspoons vanilla extract
2 eggs
2 tablespoons light corn syrup
2¹/₂ cups all-purpose flour
¹/₂ cup HERSHEY'S Cocoa
¹/₂ teaspoon baking soda
¹/₄ teaspoon salt
Decorating icing

1. Beat butter, sugar and vanilla in large bowl on medium speed of mixer until fluffy. Add eggs; beat well. Beat in corn syrup.

2. Combine flour, cocoa, baking soda and salt; gradually add to butter mixture, beating until well blended. Cover; refrigerate until dough is firm enough to handle.

3. Heat oven to 350°F. Shape dough into X and O shapes.* Place on ungreased cookie sheet.

4. Bake 5 minutes or until set. Remove from cookie sheet to wire rack. Cool completely. Decorate as desired with icing.

Makes about 5 dozen cookies

*To shape X's: Shape rounded teaspoons of dough into 3-inch logs. Place 1 log on cookie sheet; press lightly in center. Place another 3-inch log on top of first one, forming X shape. To shape O's: Shape rounded teaspoon dough into 5-inch logs. Connect ends, pressing lightly, forming O shape.

 To soften butter or margarine quickly, cut it into small chunks and place in a microwave-safe bowl. Microwave at MEDIUM for 30 seconds.

mexican chocolate macaroons

   1 package (8 ounces) semisweet baking chocolate, divided
1¾ cups plus ⅓ cup whole almonds, divided
  ¾ cup sugar
   1 teaspoon ground cinnamon
   1 teaspoon vanilla
   2 egg whites

1. Preheat oven to 400°F. Grease baking sheets; set aside.

2. Place 5 squares chocolate in food processor; process until coarsely chopped. Add 1¾ cups almonds and sugar; process using on/off pulses until mixture is finely ground. Add cinnamon, vanilla and egg whites; process just until mixture forms moist dough.

3. Shape dough into 1-inch balls (dough will be sticky). Place about 2 inches apart on prepared baking sheets. Press 1 almond on top of each cookie.

4. Bake 8 to 10 minutes or just until set. Cool 2 minutes on baking sheets. Remove cookies from baking sheets to wire racks. Cool completely.

5. Heat remaining 3 squares chocolate in small saucepan over very low heat until melted. Spoon chocolate into small resealable plastic food storage bag. Cut small corner off bottom of bag with scissors. Drizzle chocolate over cookies. *Makes 3 dozen cookies*

tip: For longer storage, allow cookies to stand until chocolate drizzle is set. Store in airtight containers.

reese's® chewy chocolate cookies

2 cups all-purpose flour
¾ cup HERSHEY'S Cocoa
1 teaspoon baking soda
½ teaspoon salt
1¼ cups (2½ sticks) butter or margarine, softened
2 cups sugar
2 eggs
2 teaspoons vanilla extract
1⅔ cups (10-ounce package) REESE'S® Peanut Butter Chips

1. Heat oven to 350°F. Stir together flour, cocoa, baking soda and salt; set aside.

2. Beat butter and sugar in large bowl with mixer until fluffy. Add eggs and vanilla; beat well. Gradually add flour mixture, beating well. Stir in peanut butter chips. Drop by rounded teaspoons onto ungreased cookie sheet.

3. Bake 8 to 9 minutes. (Do not overbake; cookies will be soft. They will puff while baking and flatten while cooling.) Cool slightly; remove from cookie sheet to wire rack. Cool completely.

Makes about 4½ dozen cookies

double chocolate banana cookies

3 to 4 extra-ripe medium DOLE® Bananas
2 cups rolled oats
2 cups sugar
1¾ cups all-purpose flour
½ cup unsweetened cocoa powder
1 teaspoon baking soda
½ teaspoon salt
1¼ cups margarine, melted
2 eggs, lightly beaten
2 cups semisweet chocolate chips
1 cup chopped natural almonds, toasted

• Purée bananas in blender; measure 2 cups for recipe.

• Combine oats, sugar, flour, cocoa, baking soda and salt until well mixed. Stir in bananas, margarine and eggs until blended. Stir in chocolate chips and almonds.

- Refrigerate batter 1 hour or until mixture becomes partially firm (batter runs during baking if too soft).

- Preheat oven to 350°F. Measure ¼-cup batter for each cookie; drop onto greased cookie sheet. Flatten slightly with spatula.

- Bake 15 to 17 minutes until cookies are golden brown. Remove to wire rack to cool.   *Makes about 2½ dozen (3-inch) cookies*

Prep Time: 15 minutes
Chill Time: 1 hour
Bake Time: 17 minutes per batch

chocolate bursts

    6 squares (1 ounce each) semisweet chocolate
    ½ cup (1 stick) I CAN'T BELIEVE IT'S NOT BUTTER!® Spread
    ¾ cup sugar
    2 eggs
    ⅓ cup all-purpose flour
    ¼ cup unsweetened cocoa powder
 1½ teaspoons vanilla extract
    1 teaspoon baking powder
    ¼ teaspoon salt
    2 cups coarsely chopped pecans or walnuts
    1 cup semisweet chocolate chips

Preheat oven to 325°F. Grease baking sheets; set aside.

In medium microwave-safe bowl, heat chocolate squares and I Can't Believe It's Not Butter! Spread on HIGH (Full Power) 1 to 2 minutes or until chocolate is almost melted. Stir until completely melted.

In large bowl, with electric mixer, beat sugar and eggs until light and ribbony, about 2 minutes. Beat in chocolate mixture, flour, cocoa, vanilla, baking powder and salt, scraping side occasionally, until well blended. Stir in nuts and chocolate chips. Drop dough by rounded tablespoonfuls onto prepared sheets, about 2 inches apart.

Bake 15 minutes or until cookies are just set. On wire rack, let stand 2 minutes; remove from sheets and cool completely.

Makes about 3 dozen cookies

brownie turtle cookies

2 squares (1 ounce each) unsweetened baking chocolate
$\frac{1}{3}$ cup solid vegetable shortening
1 cup granulated sugar
$\frac{1}{2}$ teaspoon vanilla extract
2 large eggs
1$\frac{1}{4}$ cups all-purpose flour
$\frac{1}{2}$ teaspoon baking powder
$\frac{1}{2}$ teaspoon salt
1 cup "M&M's"® Milk Chocolate Mini Baking Bits, divided
1 cup pecan halves
$\frac{1}{3}$ cup caramel ice cream topping
$\frac{1}{3}$ cup shredded coconut
$\frac{1}{3}$ cup finely chopped pecans

Preheat oven to 350°F. Lightly grease cookie sheets; set aside. Heat chocolate and shortening in 2-quart saucepan over low heat, stirring constantly until melted; remove from heat. Mix in sugar, vanilla and eggs. Blend in flour, baking powder and salt. Stir in $\frac{2}{3}$ cup "M&M's"® Milk Chocolate Mini Baking Bits. For each cookie, arrange 3 pecan halves, with ends almost touching at center, on prepared cookie sheets. Drop dough by rounded teaspoonfuls onto center of each group of pecans; mound the dough slightly. Bake 8 to 10 minutes just until set. *Do not overbake.* Cool completely on wire racks. In small bowl combine ice cream topping, coconut and chopped nuts; top each cookie with about 1$\frac{1}{2}$ teaspoons mixture. Press remaining $\frac{1}{3}$ cup "M&M's"® Milk Chocolate Mini Baking Bits into topping.

Makes about 2$\frac{1}{2}$ dozen cookies

chocolate almond biscotti

3 cups all-purpose flour
$^1/_2$ cup unsweetened cocoa
2 teaspoons baking powder
$^1/_2$ teaspoon salt
1 cup granulated sugar
$^2/_3$ cup FLEISCHMANN'S® Original Margarine, softened
$^3/_4$ cup EGG BEATERS® Healthy Real Egg Product
1 teaspoon almond extract
$^1/_2$ cup whole blanched almonds, toasted and coarsely chopped
   Powdered Sugar Glaze (recipe follows)

In medium bowl, combine flour, cocoa, baking powder and salt; set aside.

In large bowl, with electric mixer at medium speed, beat granulated sugar and margarine for 2 minutes or until creamy. Add Egg Beaters® and almond extract; beat well. With electric mixer at low speed, gradually add flour mixture, beating just until blended; stir in almonds.

On lightly greased baking sheet, form dough into two (12×2$^1/_2$-inch) logs. Bake at 350°F for 25 to 30 minutes or until toothpick inserted in centers comes out clean. Remove from sheet; cool on wire racks 15 minutes.

Using serrated knife, slice each log diagonally into 12 (1-inch-thick) slices; place, cut-sides up, on same baking sheet. Bake at 350°F for 12 to 15 minutes on each side or until cookies are crisp and edges are browned. Remove from sheet; cool completely on wire rack. Drizzle tops with Powdered Sugar Glaze. *Makes 2 dozen cookies*

powdered sugar glaze: In small bowl, combine 1 cup powdered sugar and 5 to 6 teaspoons water until smooth.

Prep Time: 25 minutes
Cook Time: 45 minutes

super chocolate cookies

    2 cups all-purpose flour
    $^{1}/_{3}$ cup unsweetened cocoa powder
    1 teaspoon baking soda
    $^{1}/_{2}$ teaspoon salt
  1 $^{1}/_{3}$ cups packed brown sugar
    $^{1}/_{2}$ cup (1 stick) butter, softened
    $^{1}/_{2}$ cup shortening
    2 eggs
    2 teaspoons vanilla
    1 cup candy-coated chocolate pieces
    1 cup raisins
    $^{3}/_{4}$ cup salted peanuts, coarsely chopped

1. Preheat oven to 350°F. Combine flour, cocoa, baking soda and salt in medium bowl; set aside.

2. Beat brown sugar, butter and shortening at medium speed of electric mixer until light and fluffy. Beat in eggs and vanilla until well blended. Gradually add flour mixture, beating at low speed until blended. Stir in candy pieces, raisins and peanuts.

3. Drop dough by $^{1}/_{4}$ cupfuls onto ungreased cookie sheets, spacing 3 inches apart. Flatten slightly with fingertips. Bake cookies 13 to 15 minutes or until almost set. Cool 2 minutes on cookie sheets. Transfer to wire racks. Cool completely.

Makes about 20 (4-inch) cookies

fudgey german chocolate sandwich cookies

1³/₄ cups all-purpose flour
1¹/₂ cups sugar
³/₄ cup (1¹/₂ sticks) butter or margarine, softened
²/₃ cup HERSHEY'S Cocoa or HERSHEY'S Dutch Processed Cocoa
³/₄ teaspoon baking soda
¹/₄ teaspoon salt
2 eggs
2 tablespoons milk
1 teaspoon vanilla extract
¹/₂ cup finely chopped pecans
Coconut and Pecan Filling (recipe follows)

1. Heat oven to 350°F. Combine flour, sugar, butter, cocoa, baking soda, salt, eggs, milk and vanilla in large bowl. Beat at medium speed of mixer until blended (batter will be stiff). Stir in pecans.

2. Form dough into 1¹/₄-inch balls. Place on ungreased cookie sheet; flatten slightly.

3. Bake 9 to 11 minutes or until almost set. Cool slightly; remove from cookie sheet to wire rack. Cool completely. Spread about 1 heaping tablespoon Coconut and Pecan Filling onto bottom of one cookie. Top with second cookie to make sandwich. Serve warm or at room temperature. *Makes about 17 sandwich cookies*

coconut and pecan filling

¹/₂ cup (1 stick) butter or margarine
¹/₂ cup packed light brown sugar
¹/₄ cup light corn syrup
1 cup MOUNDS® Sweetened Coconut Flakes, toasted*
1 cup finely chopped pecans
1 teaspoon vanilla extract

To toast coconut: Heat oven to 350°F. Spread coconut in even layer on baking sheet. Bake 6 to 8 minutes, stirring occasionally, until golden.

Melt butter in medium saucepan over medium heat; add brown sugar and corn syrup. Stir constantly, until thick and bubbly. Remove from heat; stir in coconut, pecans and vanilla. Use warm.

Makes about 2 cups filling

cocoa hazelnut macaroons

$\frac{1}{3}$ **cup hazelnuts**
$\frac{3}{4}$ **cup quick oats**
$\frac{1}{3}$ **cup brown sugar**
$\frac{1}{4}$ **cup plus 2 tablespoons unsweetened cocoa powder**
 2 **tablespoons all-purpose flour**
 4 **egg whites**
 1 **teaspoon vanilla**
$\frac{1}{2}$ **teaspoon salt**
$\frac{1}{3}$ **cup plus 1 tablespoon granulated sugar**

1. Preheat oven to 375°F. Spread hazelnuts in even layer on cookie sheet. Bake 8 minutes or until lightly browned. Quickly transfer nuts to clean dry dish towel. Fold towel; rub vigorously to remove as much of the skins as possible. Finely chop nuts using food processor or chef's knife. Combine with oats, brown sugar, cocoa and flour in medium bowl; mix well.

2. Reduce oven temperature to 325°F. Combine egg whites, vanilla and salt in clean dry medium mixing bowl. Beat at high speed of electric mixer until soft peaks form. Gradually add granulated sugar; continue to beat on high until stiff peaks form. Gently fold in hazelnut mixture with rubber spatula.

3. Drop dough by level measuring tablespoonfuls onto cookie sheet. Bake 15 to 17 minutes or until tops of cookies are no longer shiny. Remove to wire rack; cool completely. Store in loosely covered container. *Makes 3 dozen cookies*

 Before beating egg whites, always check that the bowl and beaters are clean and dry. The smallest trace of yolk, fat or water can prevent the whites from obtaining maximum volume. Do not use plastic bowls, because they may have an oily film even after repeated washings.

caramel nut chocolate cookies

1½ cups firmly packed light brown sugar
⅔ CRISCO® Stick or ⅔ cup CRISCO® all-vegetable shortening
1 tablespoon water
1 teaspoon vanilla
2 eggs
1¾ cups all-purpose flour
⅓ cup unsweetened cocoa powder
½ teaspoon salt
¼ teaspoon baking soda
2 cups (12 ounces) miniature semisweet chocolate chips
1 cup chopped pecans
20 to 25 caramels, unwrapped and halved

1. Heat oven to 375°F. Place sheets of foil on countertop for cooling cookies.

2. Place brown sugar, shortening, water and vanilla in large bowl. Beat at medium speed of electric mixer until well blended. Add eggs; beat well.

3. Combine flour, cocoa, salt and baking soda. Add to shortening mixture; beat at low speed just until blended. Stir in chocolate chips.

4. Shape dough into 1¼-inch balls. Dip tops in chopped pecans. Place 2 inches apart on ungreased baking sheet. Press caramel half in center of each ball.

5. Bake one baking sheet at a time at 375°F for 7 to 9 minutes or until cookies are set. *Do not overbake.* Cool 2 minutes on baking sheet. Remove cookies to foil to cool completely.

Makes about 4 dozen cookies

holiday double chocolate cookies

1 1/2 cups all-purpose flour
 1/2 cup HERSHEY'S Cocoa
 1/2 teaspoon baking soda
 1/4 teaspoon salt
 1/2 cup (1 stick) butter or margarine, softened
 3/4 cup packed light brown sugar
 1/2 cup granulated sugar
   1 teaspoon vanilla extract
   2 eggs
1 1/3 cups (10-ounce package) HERSHEY'S Semi-Sweet
     Chocolate Holiday Bits, divided

1. Heat oven to 350°F. Lightly grease cookie sheet.

2. Stir together flour, cocoa, baking soda and salt. Beat butter, brown sugar, granulated sugar and vanilla in large bowl until well blended. Add eggs; beat well. Gradually add flour mixture, blending well. Stir in 1 cup bits. Drop by rounded teaspoons onto prepared cookie sheet. Press 8 to 9 of remaining bits on dough before baking.

3. Bake 7 to 9 minutes or until cookies are set. Do not overbake. Cool slightly; remove from cookie sheet to wire rack. Cool completely.

Makes about 3 1/2 dozen cookies

chunky pecan pie bars

Crust
- 1½ cups all-purpose flour
- ½ cup (1 stick) butter or margarine, softened
- ¼ cup packed brown sugar

Filling
- 3 large eggs
- ¾ cup corn syrup
- ¾ cup granulated sugar
- 2 tablespoons butter or margarine, melted
- 1 teaspoon vanilla extract
- 1¾ cups (11.5-ounce package) NESTLÉ® TOLL HOUSE® Semi-Sweet Chocolate Chunks
- 1½ cups coarsely chopped pecans

PREHEAT oven to 350°F. Grease 13×9-inch baking pan.

For Crust

BEAT flour, butter and brown sugar in small mixer bowl until crumbly. Press into prepared baking pan.

BAKE for 12 to 15 minutes or until lightly browned.

For Filling

BEAT eggs, corn syrup, granulated sugar, butter and vanilla extract in medium bowl with wire whisk. Stir in chunks and nuts. Pour evenly over baked crust.

BAKE for 25 to 30 minutes or until set. Cool completely in pan on wire rack. Cut into bars. *Makes 2 to 3 dozen bars*

chocolate chip candy cookie bars

1²/₃ cups all-purpose flour
2 tablespoons plus 1¹/₂ cups sugar, divided
³/₄ teaspoon baking powder
1 cup (2 sticks) cold butter or margarine, divided
1 egg, slightly beaten
¹/₂ cup plus 2 tablespoons (5-ounce can) evaporated milk, divided
2 cups (12-ounce package) HERSHEY'S Semi-Sweet Chocolate Chips, divided
¹/₂ cup light corn syrup
1¹/₂ cups sliced almonds

1. Heat oven to 375°F.

2. Stir together flour, 2 tablespoons sugar and baking powder in medium bowl; using pastry blender, cut in ¹/₂ cup butter until mixture forms coarse crumbs. Stir in egg and 2 tablespoons evaporated milk; stir until mixture holds together in ball shape. Press onto bottom and ¹/₄ inch up sides of 15¹/₂×10¹/₂×1-inch jelly-roll pan.

3. Bake 8 to 10 minutes or until lightly browned; remove from oven, leaving oven on. Sprinkle 1¹/₂ cups chocolate chips evenly over crust; do not disturb chips.

4. Place remaining 1¹/₂ cups sugar, remaining ¹/₂ cup butter, remaining ¹/₂ cup evaporated milk and corn syrup in 3-quart saucepan. Cook over medium heat, stirring constantly, until mixture boils; stir in almonds. Continue cooking and stirring to 240°F on candy thermometer (soft-ball stage) or until small amount of mixture, when dropped into very cold water, forms a soft ball which flattens when removed from water. (Bulb of candy thermometer should not rest on bottom of saucepan.) Remove from heat. Immediately spoon almond mixture evenly over chips and crust; do not spread.

5. Bake 10 to 15 minutes or just until almond mixture is golden brown. Remove from oven; cool 5 minutes. Sprinkle remaining ¹/₂ cup chips over top; cool completely. Cut into bars.

Makes about 48 bars

white chocolate squares →

 1 (12-ounce) package white chocolate chips, divided
 ¼ cup (½ stick) butter or margarine
 1 (14-ounce) can EAGLE BRAND® Sweetened Condensed Milk
     (NOT evaporated milk)
 1 egg
 1 teaspoon vanilla extract
 2 cups all-purpose flour
 ½ teaspoon baking powder
 1 cup chopped pecans, toasted
   Powdered sugar

1. Preheat oven to 350°F. Grease 13×9-inch baking pan. In large saucepan over low heat, melt 1 cup chips and butter. Stir in Eagle Brand, egg and vanilla. Stir in flour and baking powder until blended. Stir in pecans and remaining chips. Spoon mixture into prepared pan.

2. Bake 20 to 25 minutes. Cool. Sprinkle with powdered sugar; cut into squares. Store covered at room temperature.   *Makes 24 squares*

Prep Time: 15 minutes
Bake Time: 20 to 25 minutes

nutty chocolate chunk bars

 3 eggs
 1 cup DOMINO® Granulated Sugar
 1 cup DOMINO® Brown Sugar, packed
 1 cup oat bran
 1 cup crunchy peanut butter
 ¾ cup butter, softened
 2 teaspoons baking soda
 2 teaspoons vanilla
 3½ cups quick-cooking oats
 1 package (12 ounces) semi-sweet chocolate chunks
 1 cup Spanish peanuts

In large bowl, beat eggs, granulated sugar and brown sugar. Add oat bran, peanut butter, butter, baking soda and vanilla. Mix well. Stir in oats, chocolate chunks and peanuts. Spread mixture into greased 15×10×2-inch pan. Bake in 350°F oven 20 to 25 minutes.

Makes 36 bars

peanutty gooey bars

Crust

 2 cups chocolate graham cracker crumbs
 ¹/₂ cup (1 stick) butter or margarine, melted
 ¹/₃ cup granulated sugar

Topping

 1²/₃ cups (11-ounce package) NESTLÉ® TOLL HOUSE®
 Peanut Butter & Milk Chocolate Morsels, *divided*
 1 can (14 ounces) NESTLÉ® CARNATION®
 Sweetened Condensed Milk
 1 teaspoon vanilla extract
 1 cup coarsely chopped peanuts

PREHEAT oven to 350°F.

For Crust

COMBINE graham cracker crumbs, butter and sugar in medium bowl; press onto bottom of ungreased 13×9-inch baking pan.

For Topping

MICROWAVE *1 cup* morsels, sweetened condensed milk and vanilla extract in medium, uncovered, microwave-safe bowl on HIGH (100%) power for 1 minute. STIR. Morsels may retain some of their original shape. If necessary, microwave at additional 10- to 15-second intervals, stirring until morsels are melted. Pour evenly over crust. Top with nuts and *remaining* morsels.

BAKE for 20 to 25 minutes or until edges are bubbly. Cool completely in pan on wire rack. Cut into bars. *Makes 2 dozen bars*

 To melt butter quickly and easily, place one stick of butter in a microwavable dish. Cover with plastic wrap and microwave at HIGH 1 to 1¹/₂ minutes.

marvelous cookie bars

$^1/_2$ cup (1 stick) butter or margarine, softened
1 cup firmly packed light brown sugar
2 large eggs
$1^1/_3$ cups all-purpose flour
1 cup quick-cooking or old-fashioned oats, uncooked
$^1/_3$ cup unsweetened cocoa powder
1 teaspoon baking powder
$^1/_2$ teaspoon salt
$^1/_4$ teaspoon baking soda
$^1/_2$ cup chopped walnuts, divided
1 cup "M&M's"® Semi-Sweet Chocolate Mini Baking Bits, divided
$^1/_2$ cup cherry preserves
$^1/_4$ cup shredded coconut

Preheat oven to 350°F. Lightly grease 9×9×2-inch baking pan; set aside. In large bowl cream butter and sugar until light and fluffy; beat in eggs. In medium bowl combine flour, oats, cocoa powder, baking powder, salt and baking soda; blend into creamed mixture. Stir in $^1/_4$ cup nuts and $^3/_4$ cup "M&M's"® Semi-Sweet Chocolate Mini Baking Bits. Reserve 1 cup dough; spread remaining dough into prepared pan. Combine preserves, coconut and remaining $^1/_4$ cup nuts; spread evenly over dough to within $^1/_2$ inch of edge. Drop reserved dough by rounded teaspoonfuls over preserves mixture; sprinkle with remaining $^1/_4$ cup "M&M's"® Semi-Sweet Chocolate Mini Baking Bits. Bake 25 to 30 minutes or until slightly firm near edges. Cool completely. Cut into bars. Store in tightly covered container.   *Makes 16 bars*

chocolate cream cheese sugar cookie bars

1 package (22.3 ounces) golden sugar cookie mix
3 eggs, divided
¹/₃ cup plus 6 tablespoons butter or margarine, softened and divided
1 teaspoon water
1 package (8 ounces) cream cheese, softened
1 package (3 ounces) cream cheese, softened
³/₄ cup granulated sugar
¹/₃ cup HERSHEY'S Cocoa
1¹/₂ teaspoons vanilla extract
Powdered sugar

1. Heat oven to 350°F.

2. Empty cookie mix into large bowl. Break up any lumps. Add 2 eggs, ¹/₃ cup butter and water; stir with spoon or fork until well blended. Spread into ungreased 13×9×2-inch baking pan.

3. Beat cream cheese and remaining 6 tablespoons butter in medium bowl on medium speed of mixer until fluffy. Stir together granulated sugar and cocoa; gradually add to cream cheese mixture, beating until smooth and well blended. Add remaining egg and vanilla; beat well. Spread cream cheese mixture evenly over cookie batter.

4. Bake 35 to 40 minutes or until no imprint remains when touched lightly in center. Cool completely in pan on wire rack. Sprinkle powdered sugar over top. Cut into bars. Cover; store leftover bars in refrigerator. *Makes about 24 to 30 bars*

chocolate nut bars →

1¾ cups graham cracker crumbs
½ cup (1 stick) butter or margarine, melted
1 (14-ounce) can EAGLE BRAND® Sweetened Condensed Milk
  (NOT evaporated milk)
2 cups (12 ounces) semi-sweet chocolate chips, divided
1 teaspoon vanilla extract
1 cup chopped nuts

1. Preheat oven to 375°F. In medium mixing bowl, combine crumbs and butter; press firmly on bottom of ungreased 13×9-inch baking pan. Bake 8 minutes. Reduce oven temperature to 350°F.

2. In small saucepan, melt Eagle Brand with 1 cup chips and vanilla. Spread chocolate mixture over prepared crust. Top with remaining 1 cup chips and nuts; press down firmly.

3. Bake 25 to 30 minutes. Cool. Chill, if desired. Cut into bars. Store loosely covered at room temperature.   *Makes 24 to 36 bars*

Prep Time: 10 minutes
Bake Time: 33 to 38 minutes

double chocolate fantasy bars

2 cups chocolate cookie crumbs
⅓ cup (5⅓ tablespoons) butter or margarine, melted
1 (14-ounce) can sweetened condensed milk
1¾ cups "M&M's"® Semi-Sweet Chocolate Mini Baking Bits
1 cup shredded coconut
1 cup chopped walnuts or pecans

Preheat oven to 350°F. In large bowl combine cookie crumbs and butter; press mixture onto bottom of 13×9×2-inch baking pan. Pour condensed milk evenly over crumbs. Combine "M&M's"® Semi-Sweet Chocolate Mini Baking Bits, coconut and nuts. Sprinkle mixture evenly over condensed milk; press down lightly. Bake 25 to 30 minutes or until set. Cool completely. Cut into bars. Store in tightly covered container.   *Makes 32 bars*

chocolate peanutty crumble bars

  $1/2$ cup butter or margarine
  1 cup all-purpose flour
  $3/4$ cup instant oats, uncooked
  $1/3$ cup firmly packed brown sugar
  $1/2$ teaspoon baking soda
  $1/2$ teaspoon vanilla extract
  4 SNICKERS® Bars (2.07 ounces each), cut into 8 slices each

Preheat oven to 350°F. Grease bottom of 8-inch square pan. Melt butter in large saucepan. Remove from heat; stir in flour, oats, brown sugar, baking soda and vanilla. Blend until crumbly. Press $2/3$ of the mixture into prepared pan. Arrange SNICKERS® Bar slices in pan over crust, about $1/2$ inch from edge of pan. Finely crumble remaining flour mixture over sliced SNICKERS® Bars. Bake for 25 minutes or until edges are golden brown. Cool in pan on cooling rack. Cut into bars or squares to serve.

Makes 24 bars

white chocolate cranberry cookie bars

  2 cups all-purpose flour
  1 teaspoon baking powder
  1 teaspoon salt
  $1^{3}/4$ cups sugar
  4 eggs
  1 teaspoon vanilla extract
  1 bag (12 ounces) white chocolate chips (2 cups), divided
  $1/2$ cup (1 stick) IMPERIAL® Spread
  1 cup dried cranberries

Preheat oven to 350°F. Grease 13×9-inch baking pan; set aside. In medium bowl, combine flour, baking powder and salt; set aside. In small bowl, with wire whisk, beat sugar, eggs and vanilla; set aside.

In medium saucepan, melt 1 cup white chocolate chips with spread over low heat, stirring occasionally. Remove from heat; let cool slightly. While stirring chocolate mixture, slowly stir in egg mixture, then flour mixture until blended. Stir in remaining 1 cup chips and cranberries. Evenly pour into prepared pan.

Bake uncovered 40 minutes or until center springs back when lightly touched. On wire rack, cool completely. To serve, cut into bars.

Makes 2 dozen bars

toffee brownie bars

Crust
- ³/₄ cup butter or margarine, softened
- ³/₄ cup firmly packed brown sugar
- 1 egg yolk
- ³/₄ teaspoon vanilla extract
- 1¹/₂ cups all-purpose flour

Filling
- 1 (21-ounce) package DUNCAN HINES® Family-Style Chewy Fudge Brownie Mix
- 1 egg
- ¹/₃ cup water
- ¹/₃ cup vegetable oil

Topping
- 1 package (12 ounces) milk chocolate chips, melted
- ³/₄ cup finely chopped pecans

1. Preheat oven to 350°F. Grease 15¹/₂×10¹/₂×1-inch pan.

2. For crust, combine butter, brown sugar, egg yolk and vanilla extract in large bowl. Stir in flour. Spread in prepared pan. Bake at 350°F for 15 minutes or until golden.

3. For filling, prepare brownie mix with egg, water and oil following package directions. Spread over hot crust. Bake at 350°F for 15 minutes or until surface appears set. Cool 30 minutes.

4. For topping, spread melted chocolate on top of brownie layer; sprinkle with pecans. Cool completely. *Makes 48 bars*

tip: Bars can be made ahead and frozen in an airtight container for several weeks.

spiced chocolate pecan squares

Cookie Base
- 1 cup all-purpose flour
- $^1/_2$ cup packed light brown sugar
- $^1/_2$ teaspoon baking soda
- $^1/_4$ cup ($^1/_2$ stick) butter or margarine, softened

Topping
- 1 package (8 ounces) semi-sweet chocolate baking squares
- 2 large eggs
- $^1/_4$ cup packed light brown sugar
- $^1/_4$ cup light corn syrup
- 2 tablespoons *French's*® Worcestershire Sauce
- 1 tablespoon vanilla extract
- $1^1/_2$ cups chopped pecans or walnuts, divided

Preheat oven to 375°F. To prepare cookie base, place flour, $^1/_2$ cup sugar and baking soda in food processor or bowl of electric mixer. Process or mix 10 seconds. Add butter. Process or beat 30 seconds or until mixture resembles fine crumbs. Press evenly into bottom of greased 9-inch baking pan. Bake 15 minutes.

Meanwhile, to prepare topping, place chocolate in microwave-safe bowl. Microwave, uncovered, on HIGH 2 minutes or until chocolate is melted, stirring until chocolate is smooth; set aside.

Place eggs, $^1/_4$ cup sugar, corn syrup, Worcestershire and vanilla in food processor or bowl of electric mixer. Process or beat until well blended. Add melted chocolate. Process or beat until smooth. Stir in 1 cup nuts. Pour chocolate mixture over cookie base. Sprinkle with remaining $^1/_2$ cup nuts. Bake 40 minutes or until toothpick inserted into center comes out with slightly fudgy crumbs. (Cookie will be slightly puffed along edges.) Cool completely on wire rack. To serve, cut into squares.

Makes 16 servings

Prep Time: 20 minutes
Cook Time: 55 minutes

emily's dream bars

$^1/_2$ Butter Flavor CRISCO® Stick or $^1/_2$ cup Butter Flavor CRISCO®
  all-vegetable shortening plus additional for greasing
1 cup JIF® Crunchy Peanut Butter
$^1/_2$ cup firmly packed brown sugar
$^1/_2$ cup light corn syrup
1 egg
1 teaspoon vanilla
1 cup all-purpose flour
$^1/_2$ teaspoon baking powder
$^1/_4$ cup milk
2 cups 100% natural oats, honey and raisins cereal
1 package (12 ounces) miniature semisweet chocolate chips
  (2 cups), divided
1 cup almond brickle chips
1 cup milk chocolate covered peanuts
1 package (2 ounces) nut topping ($^1/_3$ cup)

1. Heat oven to 350°F. Grease 13×9×2-inch pan with shortening. Place wire rack on countertop for cooling bars.

2. Combine $^1/_2$ cup shortening, peanut butter, brown sugar and corn syrup in large bowl. Beat at medium speed of electric mixer until creamy. Add egg and vanilla. Beat well.

3. Combine flour and baking powder. Add alternately with milk to creamed mixture at medium speed. Stir in cereal, 1 cup chocolate chips, almond brickle chips and chocolate covered nuts with spoon. Spread in prepared pan.

4. Bake at 350°F for 20 to 26 minutes or until golden brown and toothpick inserted in center comes out clean. *Do not overbake.* Sprinkle remaining 1 cup chocolate chips over top immediately after removing from oven. Remove pan to wire rack. Let stand about 3 minutes or until chips become shiny and soft. Spread over top. Sprinkle with nut topping. Cool completely. Cut into 2×1-inch bars.

Makes 4$^1/_2$ dozen bars

caramel oatmeal chewies

1¾ cups quick or old-fashioned oats
1¾ cups all-purpose flour, *divided*
¾ cup packed brown sugar
½ teaspoon baking soda
¼ teaspoon salt (optional)
¾ cup (1½ sticks) butter or margarine, melted
2 cups (12-ounce package) NESTLÉ® TOLL HOUSE®
   Semi-Sweet Chocolate Morsels
1 cup chopped nuts
1 cup caramel ice-cream topping

PREHEAT oven to 350°F. Grease bottom of 13×9-inch baking pan.

COMBINE oats, *1½ cups* flour, brown sugar, baking soda and salt in large bowl. Stir in butter; mix well. Reserve *1 cup* oat mixture; press *remaining* oat mixture onto bottom of prepared baking pan.

BAKE for 12 to 15 minutes or until golden brown. Sprinkle with morsels and nuts. Mix caramel topping with *remaining* flour in small bowl; drizzle over morsels to within ¼ inch of pan edges. Sprinkle with *reserved* oat mixture.

BAKE for 18 to 22 minutes or until golden brown. Cool in pan on wire rack; refrigerate until firm.   *Makes about 2½ dozen bars*

chocolate & malt bars

1 cup all-purpose flour
1 cup malted milk powder or malted milk drink mix
2 teaspoons baking powder
$\frac{1}{4}$ teaspoon salt
$\frac{1}{2}$ cup granulated sugar
$\frac{1}{4}$ cup firmly packed light brown sugar
$\frac{1}{4}$ cup ($\frac{1}{2}$ stick) butter, softened
$\frac{1}{2}$ cup milk
$\frac{1}{2}$ teaspoon vanilla extract
2 large eggs
1 cup "M&M's"® Chocolate Mini Baking Bits, divided
Chocolate Malt Frosting (recipe follows)

Preheat oven to 350°F. Lightly grease 13×9-inch baking pan; set aside. In large bowl combine flour, malted milk powder, baking powder and salt; stir in sugars. Beat in butter, milk and vanilla; blend well. Add eggs; beat 2 minutes. Spread batter in prepared pan. Sprinkle with $\frac{1}{4}$ cup "M&M's"® Chocolate Mini Baking Bits. Bake about 20 minutes or until toothpick inserted in center comes out clean. Cool completely on wire rack. Prepare Chocolate Malt Frosting; spread over bars in pan. Sprinkle with remaining $\frac{3}{4}$ cup "M&M's"® Chocolate Mini Baking Bits. Store in tightly covered container.   *Makes 2 dozen bars*

chocolate malt frosting

$\frac{1}{4}$ cup ($\frac{1}{2}$ stick) butter, softened
4 teaspoons light corn syrup
$\frac{1}{2}$ teaspoon vanilla extract
3 tablespoons unsweetened cocoa powder
$\frac{1}{4}$ cup malted milk powder or malted milk drink mix
1$\frac{1}{2}$ cups powdered sugar
3 to 4 tablespoons milk

In small bowl beat butter, corn syrup and vanilla; add cocoa powder and malted milk powder until well blended. Blend in powdered sugar and enough milk for good spreading consistency.

chocolate chips and raspberry bars

1½ cups all-purpose flour
½ cup sugar
½ teaspoon baking powder
½ teaspoon salt
½ cup (1 stick) butter or margarine, softened
1 egg, beaten
¼ cup milk
¼ teaspoon vanilla extract
¾ cup raspberry preserves
1 cup HERSHEY'S Semi-Sweet Chocolate Chips

1. Heat oven to 400°F. Grease 13×9×2-inch baking pan.

2. Stir together flour, sugar, baking powder and salt in large bowl. Cut in butter with pastry blender or two knives until mixture resembles coarse crumbs. Add egg, milk and vanilla; beat on medium speed of mixer until well blended.

3. Reserve ½ cup mixture for topping. Spread remaining mixture onto bottom of prepared pan (this will be a very thin layer). Spread preserves evenly over batter; sprinkle chocolate chips over top. Drop reserved batter by ½ teaspoons over chips.

4. Bake 25 minutes or until golden. Cool completely in pan on wire rack. Cut into bars. *Makes about 32 bars*

tip: Rich, buttery bar cookies and brownies freeze extremely well. Freeze in airtight containers or freezer bags for up to three months. Thaw at room temperature.

world's best.
brownies

hershey's best brownies

1 cup (2 sticks) butter or margarine
2 cups sugar
2 teaspoons vanilla extract
4 eggs
³/₄ cup HERSHEY'S Cocoa or HERSHEY'S Dutch Processed Cocoa
1 cup all-purpose flour
¹/₂ teaspoon baking powder
¹/₄ teaspoon salt
1 cup chopped nuts (optional)

1. Heat oven to 350°F. Grease 13×9×2-inch baking pan.

2. Place butter in large microwave-safe bowl. Microwave at HIGH (100%) 2 to 2¹/₂ minutes or until melted. Stir in sugar and vanilla. Add eggs, one at a time, beating well with spoon after each addition. Add cocoa; beat until well blended. Add flour, baking powder and salt; beat well. Stir in nuts, if desired. Pour batter into prepared pan.

3. Bake 30 to 35 minutes or until brownies begin to pull away from sides of pan. Cool completely in pan on wire rack. Cut into bars.

Makes about 36 brownies

layers of love chocolate brownies

¾ cup all-purpose flour
¾ cup NESTLÉ® TOLL HOUSE® Baking Cocoa
¼ teaspoon salt
½ cup (1 stick) butter, cut in pieces
½ cup granulated sugar
½ cup packed brown sugar
3 large eggs, *divided*
2 teaspoons vanilla extract
1 cup chopped pecans
¾ cup NESTLÉ® TOLL HOUSE® Premier White Morsels
½ cup caramel ice cream topping
¾ cup NESTLÉ® TOLL HOUSE® Semi-Sweet Chocolate Morsels

PREHEAT oven to 350°F. Grease 8-inch-square baking pan.

COMBINE flour, cocoa and salt in small bowl. Beat butter, granulated sugar and brown sugar in large mixer bowl until creamy. Add *2 eggs,* one at a time, beating well after each addition. Add vanilla extract; mix well. Gradually beat in flour mixture. Reserve ¾ *cup* batter. Spread *remaining* batter into prepared baking pan. Sprinkle pecans and white morsels over batter. Drizzle caramel topping over top. Beat *remaining* egg and *reserved* batter in same large bowl until light in color. Stir in semi-sweet morsels. Spread evenly over caramel topping.

BAKE for 30 to 35 minutes or until center is set. Cool completely in pan on wire rack. Cut into squares. *Makes 16 brownies*

 Brown sugar should always be firmly packed into a measuring cup before using. To test, fill the cup with brown sugar and turn it upside down. If the sugar holds its shape, it's been correctly measured.

blast-off brownies →

4 (1-ounce) squares unsweetened chocolate
3/4 cup (1 1/2 sticks) butter or margarine
2 cups sugar
1 cup flour
3 eggs
1 tablespoon TABASCO® brand Pepper Sauce
1/2 cup semisweet chocolate chips
1/2 cup walnuts, chopped

Preheat oven to 350°F. Grease 9×9-inch baking pan. Melt chocolate and butter in small saucepan over medium-low heat, stirring frequently. Combine sugar, flour, eggs, TABASCO® Sauce and melted chocolate mixture in large bowl until well blended. Stir in chocolate chips and walnuts. Spoon mixture into prepared pan. Bake 35 to 40 minutes or until toothpick inserted in center comes out clean. Cool in pan on wire rack.   *Makes 16 brownies*

peanut butter marbled brownies

4 ounces cream cheese, softened
1/2 cup peanut butter
2 tablespoons sugar
1 egg
1 package (20 to 22 ounces) brownie mix plus ingredients
    to prepare mix
3/4 cup lightly salted cocktail peanuts

1. Preheat oven to 350°F. Lightly grease 13×9-inch baking pan.

2. Beat cream cheese, peanut butter, sugar and egg in medium bowl at medium speed of electric mixer until blended.

3. Prepare brownie mix according to package directions. Spread brownie mixture evenly in prepared pan. Spoon peanut butter mixture in dollops over brownie mixture. Swirl peanut butter mixture into brownie mixture with tip of knife. Sprinkle peanuts on top; lightly press into batter.

4. Bake 30 to 35 minutes or until toothpick inserted into center comes out almost clean. (Do not overbake.) Cool brownies completely in pan on wire rack. Cut into 2-inch squares.   *Makes 2 dozen brownies*

black russian brownies

4 squares (1 ounce each) unsweetened chocolate
1 cup butter
3/4 teaspoon ground black pepper
4 eggs, lightly beaten
1 1/2 cups granulated sugar
1 1/2 teaspoons vanilla
1/3 cup KAHLÚA® Liqueur
2 tablespoons vodka
1 1/3 cups all-purpose flour
1/2 teaspoon salt
1/4 teaspoon baking powder
1 cup chopped walnuts or toasted sliced almonds
Powdered sugar (optional)

Preheat oven to 350°F. Line bottom of 13×9-inch baking pan with waxed paper. Melt chocolate and butter with pepper in small saucepan over low heat, stirring until smooth. Remove from heat; cool.

Combine eggs, granulated sugar and vanilla in large bowl; beat well. Stir in cooled chocolate mixture, Kahlúa and vodka. Combine flour, salt and baking powder; add to chocolate mixture and stir until blended. Add walnuts. Spread evenly in prepared pan.

Bake just until wooden toothpick inserted into center comes out clean, about 25 minutes. *Do not overbake.* Cool in pan on wire rack. Cut into bars. Sprinkle with powdered sugar.

Makes about 2 1/2 dozen brownies

chocolate peanut brownie bars

2 eggs
1 cup sugar
²/₃ cup butter, melted
1 teaspoon vanilla
³/₄ cup flour
¹/₃ cup unsweetened cocoa powder
1 teaspoon baking powder
¹/₂ teaspoon salt
1¹/₂ cups coarsely chopped, peeled and cored apples or Bartlett
    pears
1 cup chopped dry-roasted peanuts, divided
¹/₂ cup peanut butter morsels

Preheat oven to 350°F. Beat eggs in large bowl until fluffy. Blend in sugar, butter and vanilla, beating until sugar is dissolved.

Combine flour, cocoa, baking powder and salt in separate bowl. Stir into egg mixture until dry ingredients are just moistened. Carefully fold in apples or pears, ¹/₂ cup peanuts and peanut butter morsels.

Pour into greased 8-inch baking pan; sprinkle with remaining ¹/₂ cup peanuts. Bake 30 to 35 minutes or until toothpick inserted into center comes out clean. Remove to wire rack to cool completely. Cut into squares.   *Makes 16 bars*

Favorite recipe from **Texas Peanut Producers Board**

almond brownies

¹/₂ cup (1 stick) butter
2 squares (1 ounce each) unsweetened baking chocolate
2 large eggs
1 cup firmly packed light brown sugar
¹/₄ teaspoon almond extract
¹/₂ cup all-purpose flour
1¹/₂ cups "M&M's"® Chocolate Mini Baking Bits, divided
¹/₂ cup slivered almonds, toasted and divided
Chocolate Glaze (recipe follows)

Preheat oven to 350°F. Grease and flour 8×8×2-inch baking pan; set aside. In small saucepan melt butter and chocolate over low heat; stir to blend. Remove from heat; let cool. In medium bowl beat eggs and brown sugar until well blended; stir in chocolate mixture and almond extract. Add flour. Stir in 1 cup "M&M's"® Chocolate Mini Baking Bits and ¹/₄ cup almonds. Spread batter evenly in prepared pan. Bake 25 to 28 minutes or until firm in center. Cool completely on wire rack. Prepare Chocolate Glaze. Spread over brownies; decorate with remaining ¹/₂ cup "M&M's"® Chocolate Mini Baking Bits and remaining ¹/₄ cup almonds. Cut into bars. Store in tightly covered container. *Makes 16 brownies*

chocolate glaze: In small saucepan over low heat combine 4 teaspoons water and 1 tablespoon butter until it comes to a boil. Stir in 4 teaspoons unsweetened cocoa powder; mix well. Gradually stir in ¹/₂ cup powdered sugar until smooth. Remove from heat; stir in ¹/₄ teaspoon vanilla extract. Let glaze cool slightly.

caramel fudge brownies

1 jar (12 ounces) caramel ice cream topping
1¼ cups all-purpose flour, divided
¼ teaspoon baking powder
  Dash salt
4 squares (1 ounce each) unsweetened chocolate, coarsely
  chopped
¾ cup (1½ sticks) butter
2 cups sugar
3 eggs
2 teaspoons vanilla
¾ cup semisweet chocolate chips
¾ cup chopped pecans

1. Preheat oven to 350°F. Lightly grease 13×9-inch baking pan.

2. Combine caramel topping and ¼ cup flour in small bowl; set aside. Combine remaining 1 cup flour, baking powder and salt in small bowl; mix well.

3. Place unsweetened chocolate and butter in medium microwavable bowl. Microwave at HIGH 2 minutes or until butter is melted; stir until chocolate is completely melted.

4. Stir sugar into melted chocolate. Add eggs and vanilla; stir until combined. Add flour mixture, stirring until well blended. Spread chocolate mixture evenly in prepared pan.

5. Bake 25 minutes. Immediately after removing brownies from oven, spread caramel mixture over brownies. Sprinkle top evenly with chocolate chips and pecans.

6. Return pan to oven; bake 20 to 25 minutes or until topping is golden brown and bubbling. *Do not overbake.* Cool brownies completely in pan on wire rack. Cut into 2×1½-inch bars.

7. Store tightly covered at room temperature or freeze up to 3 months.

Makes 3 dozen brownies

brownie gems →

1 package DUNCAN HINES® Chocolate Lover's® Double Fudge
  Brownie Mix
2 eggs
2 tablespoons water
$^1/_3$ cup vegetable oil
28 miniature peanut butter cup or chocolate kiss candies
1 container of your favorite DUNCAN HINES® frosting

1. Preheat oven to 350°F. Spray (1$^3/_4$-inch) mini-muffin pans with
vegetable cooking spray or line with foil baking cups.

2. Combine brownie mix, fudge packet from mix, eggs, water
and oil in large bowl. Stir with spoon until well blended, about
50 strokes. Drop 1 heaping teaspoonful of batter into each muffin
cup; top with candy. Cover candy with more batter. Bake at 350°F
for 15 to 17 minutes.

3. Cool 5 minutes. Carefully loosen brownies from pan. Remove to
wire racks; cool completely. Frost and decorate as desired.

Makes 30 brownie gems

chocolate syrup brownies

1 egg
1 cup packed light brown sugar
$^3/_4$ cup HERSHEY'S Syrup
1$^1/_2$ cups all-purpose flour
$^1/_4$ teaspoon baking soda
  Dash salt
$^1/_2$ cup (1 stick) butter or margarine, melted
$^3/_4$ cup chopped pecans or walnuts

1. Heat oven to 350°F. Grease 9-inch square baking pan.

2. Beat egg lightly in small bowl; add brown sugar and syrup, beating
until well blended. Stir together flour, baking soda and salt; gradually
add to egg mixture, beating until blended. Stir in butter and nuts.
Spread batter into prepared pan.

3. Bake 35 to 40 minutes or until brownies begin to pull away from
sides of pan. Cool completely in pan on wire rack. Cut into squares.

Makes about 16 brownies

rocky road brownies

   1 cup HERSHEY'S Semi-Sweet Chocolate Chips
1¼ cups miniature marshmallows
  ½ cup chopped nuts
  ½ cup (1 stick) butter or margarine
  1 cup sugar
  1 teaspoon vanilla extract
  2 eggs
  ½ cup all-purpose flour
  ⅓ cup HERSHEY'S Cocoa
  ½ teaspoon baking powder
  ½ teaspoon salt

1. Heat oven to 350°F. Grease 9-inch square baking pan.

2. Stir together chocolate chips, marshmallows and nuts; set aside. Place butter in large microwave-safe bowl. Microwave at HIGH (100% power) 1 to 1½ minutes or until melted. Add sugar, vanilla and eggs, beating with spoon until well blended. Add flour, cocoa, baking powder and salt; blend well. Spread batter in prepared pan.

3. Bake 22 minutes. Sprinkle chocolate chip mixture over top. Continue baking 5 minutes or until marshmallows have softened and puffed slightly. Cool completely. With wet knife, cut into squares.

Makes about 20 brownies

If you don't use up a whole package of marshmallows for one recipe, store them in a tightly sealed plastic bag in the freezer to prevent them from drying out.

easy double chocolate chip brownies

2 cups (12-ounce package) NESTLÉ® TOLL HOUSE® Semi-Sweet Chocolate Morsels, *divided*
¹/₂ cup (1 stick) butter or margarine, cut into pieces
3 large eggs
1¹/₄ cups all-purpose flour
1 cup granulated sugar
1 teaspoon vanilla extract
¹/₄ teaspoon baking soda
¹/₂ cup chopped nuts

PREHEAT oven to 350°F. Grease 13×9-inch baking pan.

MELT *1 cup* morsels and butter in large, *heavy-duty* saucepan over low heat; stir until smooth. Remove from heat. Stir in eggs. Stir in flour, sugar, vanilla extract and baking soda. Stir in *remaining* morsels and nuts. Spread into prepared baking pan.

BAKE for 18 to 22 minutes or until wooden pick inserted in center comes out slightly sticky. Cool completely in pan on wire rack.

Makes 2 dozen brownies

triple chocolate brownies

3 squares (1 ounce each) unsweetened chocolate, coarsely
 chopped
2 squares (1 ounce each) semisweet chocolate, coarsely chopped
$\frac{1}{2}$ cup (1 stick) butter
1 cup all-purpose flour
$\frac{1}{2}$ teaspoon salt
$\frac{1}{4}$ teaspoon baking powder
$1\frac{1}{2}$ cups sugar
3 eggs
1 teaspoon vanilla
$\frac{1}{4}$ cup sour cream
$\frac{1}{2}$ cup milk chocolate chips
Powdered sugar (optional)

1. Preheat oven to 350°F. Lightly grease 13×9-inch baking pan.

2. Place unsweetened chocolate, semisweet chocolate and butter in medium microwavable bowl. Microwave at HIGH 2 minutes or until butter is melted; stir until chocolate is completely melted. Cool to room temperature.

3. Combine flour, salt and baking powder in small bowl.

4. Beat sugar, eggs and vanilla at medium speed of electric mixer until slightly thickened. Beat in chocolate mixture until well combined. Add flour mixture; beat at low speed until blended. Add sour cream; beat at low speed until combined. Stir in milk chocolate chips. Spread mixture evenly into prepared pan.

5. Bake 20 to 25 minutes or until toothpick inserted into center comes out almost clean. *Do not overbake.* Cool brownies completely in pan on wire rack. Cut into 2-inch squares. Place powdered sugar in fine-mesh strainer; sprinkle over brownies, if desired. Store tightly covered at room temperature or freeze up to 3 months.

Makes 2 dozen brownies

white chocolate brownies

6 tablespoons butter
5 squares (1 ounce each) white chocolate, divided
1 large egg
$^1\!/_2$ cup granulated sugar
$^3\!/_4$ cup all-purpose flour
$^3\!/_4$ teaspoon vanilla extract
$^1\!/_4$ teaspoon salt
1$^1\!/_4$ cups "M&M's"® Semi-Sweet Chocolate Mini Baking Bits, divided
$^1\!/_2$ cup chopped walnuts

Preheat oven to 325°F. Lightly grease 8×8×2-inch baking pan; set aside. In small saucepan melt butter and 4 squares white chocolate over low heat; stir to blend. Remove from heat; let cool slightly. In medium bowl beat egg and sugar until light; stir in white chocolate mixture, flour, vanilla and salt. Spread batter evenly in prepared pan. Sprinkle with $^3\!/_4$ cup "M&M's"® Semi-Sweet Chocolate Mini Baking Bits and walnuts. Bake 35 to 37 minutes or until firm in center. Cool completely on wire rack. Place remaining 1 square white chocolate in small microwave-safe bowl. Microwave at HIGH 20 seconds; stir. Repeat as necessary until white chocolate is completely melted, stirring at 10-second intervals. Drizzle over brownies and sprinkle with remaining $^1\!/_2$ cup "M&M's"® Semi-Sweet Chocolate Mini Baking Bits. Cut into bars. Store in tightly covered container.

Makes 16 brownies

nuggets o' gold brownies

3 ounces unsweetened baking chocolate
$^1/_4$ cup WESSON® Vegetable Oil
2 eggs
1 cup sugar
1 teaspoon vanilla extract
$^1/_4$ teaspoon salt
$^1/_2$ cup all-purpose flour
1 (3.8-ounce) BUTTERFINGER® Candy Bar, coarsely chopped

In microwave-safe measuring cup, heat chocolate 2 minutes on HIGH in microwave oven. Stir and continue heating in 30-second intervals until chocolate is completely melted. Stir in oil and set aside to cool. In mixing bowl, beat eggs until foamy. Whisk in sugar, then add vanilla and salt. Stir in chocolate mixture, then mix in flour until all ingredients are moistened. Gently fold in candy. Pour batter into greased 9-inch baking pan and bake at 350°F for 25 to 30 minutes or until edges begin to pull away from sides of pan. Cool before cutting.

Makes 20 brownies

mississippi mud brownies

1 (21-ounce) package DUNCAN HINES® Family-Style
   Chewy Fudge Brownie Mix
2 eggs
$^1/_3$ cup water
$^1/_3$ cup vegetable oil plus additional for greasing
1 jar (7 ounces) marshmallow creme
1 container DUNCAN HINES® Milk Chocolate Frosting, melted

1. Preheat oven to 350°F. Grease bottom only of 13×9-inch pan.

2. Combine brownie mix, eggs, water and oil in large bowl. Stir with spoon until well blended, about 50 strokes. Spread in pan. Bake at 350°F for 25 to 28 minutes or until set.

3. Spread marshmallow creme gently over hot brownies. Pour $1^1/_4$ cups melted milk chocolate frosting over marshmallow creme. Swirl with knife to marble. Cool completely. Cut into bars.

Makes 20 to 24 brownies

note: Store leftover melted frosting in original container. Refrigerate.

incredibly rich
cakes

chocolate banana cake

Cake

> 1 package DUNCAN HINES® Moist Deluxe® Devil's Food
>   Cake Mix
> 3 eggs
> 1⅓ cups milk
> ½ cup vegetable oil

Topping

> 1 package (4-serving size) banana cream instant pudding
>   and pie filling mix
> 1 cup milk
> 1 cup whipping cream, whipped
> 1 medium banana
>   Lemon juice
>   Chocolate sprinkles for garnish

1. Preheat oven to 350°F. Grease and flour 13×9×2-inch pan.

2. For cake, combine cake mix, eggs, milk and oil in large bowl. Beat at low speed with electric mixer until moistened. Beat at medium speed 2 minutes. Pour into pan. Bake at 350°F 35 to 38 minutes or until toothpick inserted in center comes out clean. Cool completely.

3. For topping, combine pudding mix and milk in large bowl. Stir until smooth. Fold in whipped cream. Spread on top of cooled cake. Slice banana; dip in lemon juice and arrange on top. Garnish with chocolate sprinkles. Refrigerate until ready to serve.

Makes 12 to 16 servings

tip: A wire whisk is a great utensil to use when making instant pudding. It quickly eliminates all lumps.

chocolate almond torte

    4 eggs, separated
    ½ cup (1 stick) butter or margarine, softened
    1 cup sugar
    1 teaspoon almond extract
    1 teaspoon vanilla extract
    1 cup finely chopped toasted almonds
    ¾ cup all-purpose flour
    ½ cup unsweetened cocoa
    ½ teaspoon baking powder
    ½ teaspoon baking soda
    ⅔ cup milk
        Chocolate Almond Frosting (recipe follows)

1. Line 2 (8- or 9-inch) round cake pans with waxed paper. Preheat oven to 350°F. In small mixing bowl, beat egg whites until soft peaks form; set aside.

2. In large mixing bowl, beat butter and sugar until fluffy. Add egg yolks and extracts; mix well.

3. In medium mixing bowl, combine almonds, flour, cocoa, baking powder and baking soda; add alternately with milk to butter mixture, beating well after each addition.

4. Fold in beaten egg whites. Pour into prepared pans. Bake 18 to 20 minutes or until wooden picks inserted near centers come out clean. Cool 10 minutes; remove from pans. Cool completely.

5. Prepare Chocolate Almond Frosting. Split each cake layer; fill and frost with frosting. Garnish as desired. Store covered in refrigerator.

Makes one 4-layer cake

Prep Time: 30 minutes
Bake Time: 18 to 20 minutes

chocolate almond frosting

    2 (1-ounce) squares semi-sweet chocolate, chopped
    1 (14-ounce) can EAGLE BRAND® Sweetened Condensed Milk
        (NOT evaporated milk)
    1 teaspoon almond extract

continued on page 82

1. In heavy saucepan over medium heat, melt chocolate with Eagle Brand. Cook and stir until mixture thickens, about 10 minutes.

2. Remove from heat; cool 10 minutes. Stir in almond extract; cool.

Makes about 1 1/2 cups

Prep Time: 20 minutes

chocolate squares with nutty caramel sauce

> 1 cup sugar
> 3/4 cup all-purpose flour
> 1/2 cup HERSHEY'S Dutch Processed Cocoa or HERSHEY'S Cocoa
> 1/2 teaspoon baking powder
> 1/2 teaspoon salt
> 3/4 cup vegetable oil
> 3 eggs
> 1/4 cup milk
> 1/2 teaspoon vanilla extract
> 1 bag (14 ounces) caramel candies
> 1/2 cup water
> 1 cup pecan pieces
> Sweetened whipped cream (optional)

1. Heat oven to 350°F. Grease bottom only of 8-inch square baking pan.

2. Stir together sugar, flour, cocoa, baking powder and salt in medium bowl. Add oil, eggs, milk and vanilla; beat until smooth. Pour batter into prepared pan.

3. Bake 35 to 40 minutes or until wooden pick inserted in center comes out clean. Cool completely in pan on wire rack.

4. Remove wrappers from caramels. Combine caramels and water in small saucepan. Cook over low heat, stirring occasionally, until smooth and well blended. Stir in pecans; cool until thickened slightly. Cut cake into squares; serve with warm caramel nut sauce and sweetened whipped cream, if desired. *Makes 9 servings*

chocolate lava cakes

6 tablespoons I CAN'T BELIEVE IT'S NOT BUTTER!® Spread
3 squares (1 ounce each) bittersweet or semi-sweet chocolate,
    cut into pieces
1/2 cup granulated sugar
6 tablespoons all-purpose flour
    Pinch salt
2 large eggs
2 large egg yolks
1/4 teaspoon vanilla extract
    Confectioners' sugar

Line bottom of four (4-ounce) ramekins* or custard cups with waxed paper, then grease; set aside.

In medium microwave-safe bowl, microwave I Can't Believe It's Not Butter! Spread and chocolate at HIGH (Full Power) 45 seconds or until chocolate is melted; stir until smooth. With wire whisk, beat in granulated sugar, flour and salt until blended. Beat in eggs, egg yolks and vanilla. Evenly spoon into prepared ramekins. Refrigerate 1 hour or until ready to bake.

Preheat oven to 425°F. Arrange ramekins on baking sheet. Bake 13 minutes or until edges are firm but centers are still slightly soft. Do not overbake. On wire rack, cool 5 minutes. To serve, carefully run sharp knife around cake edges. Unmold onto serving plates, then remove waxed paper. Sprinkle with confectioners' sugar and serve immediately. *Makes 4 servings*

To bake in 12-cup muffin pan, line bottoms of 8 muffin cups with waxed paper, then grease. Evenly spoon in batter. Refrigerate as above. Bake at 425°F for 9 minutes or until edges are firm but centers are still slightly soft. Do not overbake. On wire rack, cool 5 minutes. To serve, carefully run sharp knife around cake edges and gently lift out of pan. (Do not turn pan upside-down to unmold.) Arrange cakes, bottom sides up, on serving plates, 2 cakes per serving. Remove waxed paper and sprinkle as above.

triple chocolate cake

1½ cups sugar
¾ cup (1½ sticks) butter, softened
1 egg
1 teaspoon vanilla
2 cups all-purpose flour
⅔ cup unsweetened cocoa powder
2 teaspoons baking soda
¼ teaspoon salt
1 cup buttermilk
¾ cup sour cream
Chocolate Ganache Filling (recipe follows)
Easy Chocolate Frosting (recipe follows)

1. Preheat oven to 350°F. Grease and flour two 9-inch round cake pans. Beat sugar and butter at medium speed of electric mixer until light and fluffy. Beat in egg and vanilla until blended. Combine flour, cocoa, baking soda and salt in medium bowl. Add flour mixture to butter mixture alternately with buttermilk and sour cream, beginning and ending with flour mixture. Beat well after each addition. Divide batter evenly between prepared pans.

2. Bake 30 to 35 minutes or until wooden toothpick inserted in centers comes out clean. Cool in pans 10 minutes. Remove from pans to wire racks; cool completely. Cut each cake layer in half horizontally.

3. Meanwhile, prepare Chocolate Ganache Filling and Easy Chocolate Frosting. Place one cake layer on serving plate. Spread with ⅓ of filling. Repeat layers two more times. Top with remaining cake layer. Spread frosting over cake. Garnish as desired.   *Makes 1 (9-inch) layer cake*

chocolate ganache filling: Bring ¾ cup heavy cream, 1 tablespoon butter and 1 tablespoon granulated sugar to a boil; stir until sugar is dissolved. Place 1½ cups semisweet chocolate chips in medium bowl; pour cream mixture over chocolate and let stand 5 minutes. Stir until smooth; let stand 15 minutes or until filling reaches desired consistency. (Filling will thicken as it cools.) Makes about 1½ cups.

easy chocolate frosting: Beat ½ cup (1 stick) softened butter in large bowl with electric mixer at medium speed until creamy. Add 4 cups powdered sugar and ¾ cup cocoa alternately with ½ cup milk; beat until smooth. Stir in 1½ teaspoons vanilla. Makes about 3 cups.

chocolate truffle cake with strawberry sauce

Truffle Cake

1³/₄ cups (11.5-ounce package) NESTLÉ® TOLL HOUSE®
   Milk Chocolate Morsels, *divided*
¹/₂ cup (1 stick) butter
3 large eggs
²/₃ cup granulated sugar
1 teaspoon vanilla extract
¹/₄ teaspoon salt
²/₃ cup all-purpose flour

Glaze

¹/₄ cup NESTLÉ® TOLL HOUSE® Butterscotch Flavored Morsels
¹/₄ cup creamy peanut butter

Sauce

2 cups fresh or frozen strawberries, thawed
2 tablespoons granulated sugar
   Garnish suggestions: whipped topping, fresh strawberries,
   fresh mint leaves

For Truffle Cake

PREHEAT oven to 350°F. Grease and flour 9-inch springform pan. Melt *1 cup* milk chocolate morsels and butter in small, uncovered, microwave-safe bowl on MEDIUM-HIGH (70%) power for 1 minute. STIR. Morsels may retain some of their original shape. If necessary, microwave at additional 10- to 15-second intervals, stirring just until morsels are melted. Cool for 10 minutes.

BEAT eggs, ²/₃ cup sugar, vanilla extract and salt in large mixer bowl. Blend in chocolate mixture. Stir in flour; mix well. Pour into prepared pan.

BAKE for 30 to 35 minutes or until wooden pick inserted in center comes out clean. Cool completely in pan on wire rack. Remove side of pan.

For Glaze

MELT *remaining* milk chocolate morsels, butterscotch morsels and peanut butter in small, uncovered, microwave-safe bowl on MEDIUM-HIGH (70%) power for 1 minute. STIR. Morsels may retain some of their original shape. If necessary, microwave at additional 10- to 15-second intervals, stirring just until morsels are melted. Cool slightly. Spread glaze over top and side of cooled cake. Refrigerate for 30 minutes or until glaze is set.

For Strawberry Sauce
PLACE strawberries and 2 tablespoons sugar in blender; cover. Blend until smooth. Refrigerate until serving time. To serve, cut cake into wedges. Garnish with Strawberry Sauce, whipped topping, strawberries and mint leaves. *Makes 12 servings*

chocolate sheet cake

1¼ cups (2½ sticks) butter or margarine, divided
1 cup water
½ cup unsweetened cocoa, divided
2 cups all-purpose flour
1½ cups firmly packed light brown sugar
1 teaspoon baking soda
1 teaspoon ground cinnamon
½ teaspoon salt
1 (14-ounce) can EAGLE BRAND® Sweetened Condensed Milk (NOT evaporated milk), divided
2 eggs
1 teaspoon vanilla extract
1 cup powdered sugar
1 cup coarsely chopped nuts

1. Preheat oven to 350°F. In small saucepan over medium heat, melt 1 cup butter; stir in water and ¼ cup cocoa. Bring to a boil; remove from heat. In large mixing bowl, combine flour, brown sugar, baking soda, cinnamon and salt. Add cocoa mixture; beat well. Stir in ⅓ cup Eagle Brand, eggs and vanilla. Pour into greased 15×10×1-inch jelly-roll pan. Bake 15 minutes or until cake springs back when lightly touched.

2. In small saucepan over medium heat, melt remaining ¼ cup butter; add remaining ¼ cup cocoa and remaining Eagle Brand. Stir in powdered sugar and nuts. Spread over warm cake.
Makes one 15×10-inch cake

chocolate shortcakes

1 1/4 cups all-purpose flour
1/2 cup unsweetened cocoa powder
2/3 cup granulated sugar, divided
1 tablespoon baking powder
1/8 teaspoon salt
1/2 cup (1 stick) cold butter
1/2 cup milk
1 teaspoon vanilla extract
1 1/4 cups "M&M's"® Milk Chocolate Mini Baking Bits, divided
1 large egg
1 teaspoon water
1/2 cup cold whipping cream
2 cups sliced strawberries
1/3 cup chocolate syrup

Preheat oven to 425°F. In medium bowl combine flour, cocoa powder, 1/3 cup sugar, baking powder and salt. Cut in butter with pastry blender or two knives until mixture resembles coarse crumbs. Add milk and vanilla; mix just until dry ingredients are moistened. On lightly floured surface gently knead 3/4 cup "M&M's"® Milk Chocolate Mini Baking Bits into dough until evenly dispersed. Roll or pat out to 1/2-inch thickness. Cut with 3-inch round biscuit cutter; place on ungreased cookie sheet. If necessary, reroll scraps of dough in order to make six shortcakes. In small bowl combine egg and water; brush lightly over dough. Bake 12 to 14 minutes. Cool on pan 1 minute. Remove to wire racks; cool completely. In large bowl beat whipping cream until soft peaks form. Add remaining 1/3 cup sugar; beat until stiff peaks form. Reserve 1/2 cup whipped cream. Split shortcakes and place bottom of each on plate; divide strawberries evenly among shortcakes. Top with remaining whipped cream; sprinkle with 1/4 cup "M&M's"® Milk Chocolate Mini Baking Bits. Replace tops of shortcakes; drizzle with chocolate syrup. Garnish with reserved whipped cream and remaining 1/4 cup "M&M's"® Milk Chocolate Mini Baking Bits. Serve immediately. *Makes 6 servings*

chocolate hazelnut torte

1 cup hazelnuts, toasted and skins removed*
³/₄ cup sugar, divided
¹/₄ cup I CAN'T BELIEVE IT'S NOT BUTTER!® Spread
12 squares (1 ounce each) semi-sweet chocolate, divided
6 large eggs, at room temperature
¹/₄ cup brewed espresso coffee or coffee liqueur
¹/₄ cup whipping or heavy cream, heated to boiling

*Use 1 cup whole blanched almonds, toasted, instead of hazelnuts, if desired.

Preheat oven to 325°F. Grease 9-inch cake pan and line bottom with parchment or waxed paper; set aside.

In food processor or blender, process hazelnuts and ¹/₄ cup sugar until nuts are finely ground; set aside.

In top of double boiler, melt I Can't Believe It's Not Butter! Spread and 10 squares chocolate over medium heat, stirring occasionally, until smooth; set aside and let cool.

In large bowl, with electric mixer, beat eggs and remaining ¹/₂ cup sugar until thick and pale yellow, about 4 minutes. Beat in chocolate mixture and espresso. Stir in hazelnut mixture. Pour batter into prepared pan.

Bake 30 minutes or until toothpick inserted in center comes out with moist crumbs. On wire rack, cool 10 minutes; remove from pan and cool completely.

In small bowl, pour hot cream over remaining 2 squares chocolate, chopped. Stir until chocolate is melted and mixture is smooth. Pour chocolate mixture over torte to glaze. Let stand at room temperature or refrigerate until chocolate mixture is set, about 30 minutes.

Makes 8 servings

note: Torte may be frozen up to 1 month.

chocolate intensity

Cake

    4 bars (8-ounce box) NESTLÉ® TOLL HOUSE® Unsweetened
        Chocolate Baking Bars, broken into pieces
    $^1\!/_2$ cup (1 stick) butter, softened
    $1^1\!/_2$ cups granulated sugar
    3 large eggs
    2 teaspoons vanilla extract
    $^2\!/_3$ cup all-purpose flour
        Powdered sugar (optional)

Coffee Crème Anglaise Sauce

    4 large egg yolks, lightly beaten
    $^1\!/_3$ cup granulated sugar
    1 tablespoon TASTER'S CHOICE® 100% Pure Instant Coffee
    $1^1\!/_2$ cups milk
    1 teaspoon vanilla extract

PREHEAT oven to 350°F. Grease 9-inch springform pan.

For Cake

MICROWAVE baking bars in medium, microwave-safe bowl on HIGH (100%) power for 1 minute; stir. Microwave at additional 10- to 20-second intervals, stirring until smooth; cool to lukewarm.

BEAT butter, granulated sugar, eggs and vanilla extract in small mixer bowl for about 4 minutes or until thick and pale yellow. Beat in melted chocolate. Gradually beat in flour. Spread into prepared springform pan.

BAKE for 25 to 28 minutes or until wooden pick inserted in center comes out moist. Cool in pan on wire rack for 15 minutes. Loosen and remove side of pan; cool completely. Sprinkle with powdered sugar; serve with Coffee Crème Anglaise Sauce.

For Coffee Crème Anglaise Sauce

PLACE egg yolks in medium bowl. Combine granulated sugar and Taster's Choice in medium saucepan; stir in milk. Cook over medium heat, stirring constantly, until mixture comes just to a very gentle boil. Remove from heat. Gradually whisk *half* of hot milk mixture into egg yolks; return mixture to saucepan. Cook, stirring constantly, for 3 to 4 minutes or until mixture is slightly thickened. Strain into small bowl; stir in vanilla extract. Cover; refrigerate. *Makes 10 to 12 servings*

chocolate cherry torte

1 package DUNCAN HINES® Moist Deluxe® Devil's Food
  Cake Mix
1 can (21 ounces) cherry pie filling
¼ teaspoon almond extract
1 container (8 ounces) frozen whipped topping, thawed and
  divided
¼ cup toasted sliced almonds, for garnish (see Tip)

1. Preheat oven to 350°F. Grease and flour two 9-inch round cake pans.

2. Prepare, bake and cool cake following package directions for basic recipe. Combine cherry pie filling and almond extract in small bowl. Stir until blended.

3. To assemble, place one cake layer on serving plate. Spread with 1 cup whipped topping, then half the cherry pie filling mixture. Top with second cake layer. Spread remaining pie filling to within 1½ inches of cake edge. Decorate cake edge with remaining whipped topping. Garnish with sliced almonds.   *Makes 12 to 16 servings*

tip: To toast almonds, spread in a single layer on baking sheet. Bake at 325°F 4 to 6 minutes or until fragrant and golden.

hot fudge pudding cake

1¼ cups granulated sugar, divided
1 cup all-purpose flour
½ cup HERSHEY'S Cocoa, divided
2 teaspoons baking powder
¼ teaspoon salt
½ cup milk
⅓ cup butter or margarine, melted
1½ teaspoons vanilla extract
½ cup packed light brown sugar
1¼ cups hot water
    Whipped topping

1. Heat oven to 350°F.

2. Stir together ¾ cup granulated sugar, flour, ¼ cup cocoa, baking powder and salt. Stir in milk, butter and vanilla; beat until smooth. Pour batter into ungreased 9-inch square baking pan. Stir together remaining ½ cup granulated sugar, brown sugar and remaining ¼ cup cocoa; sprinkle mixture evenly over batter. Pour hot water over top. Do not stir.

3. Bake 35 to 40 minutes or until center is almost set. Let stand 15 minutes; spoon into dessert dishes, spooning sauce from bottom of pan over top. Garnish with whipped topping.

Makes about 8 servings

Prep Time: 10 minutes
Bake Time: 35 minutes
Cool Time: 15 minutes

glazed chocolate pound cake

Cake

1³/₄ Butter Flavor CRISCO® Sticks or 1³/₄ cups Butter Flavor
CRISCO® all-vegetable shortening plus additional
for greasing

3 cups granulated sugar

5 eggs

1 teaspoon vanilla

3¹/₄ cups all-purpose flour

¹/₂ cup unsweetened cocoa powder

1 teaspoon baking powder

¹/₂ teaspoon salt

1¹/₃ cups milk

1 cup miniature semisweet chocolate chips

Glaze

1 cup miniature semisweet chocolate chips

¹/₄ Butter Flavor CRISCO® Stick or ¹/₄ cup Butter Flavor CRISCO®
all-vegetable shortening

1 tablespoon light corn syrup

1. For cake, heat oven to 325°F. Grease and flour 10-inch tube pan.

2. Combine 1³/₄ cups shortening, sugar, eggs and vanilla in large bowl. Beat at low speed of electric mixer until blended, scraping bowl frequently. Beat at high speed 6 minutes, scraping bowl occasionally. Combine flour, cocoa, baking powder and salt in medium bowl. Mix in dry ingredients alternately with milk, beating after each addition until batter is smooth. Stir in 1 cup chocolate chips. Spoon into prepared pan.

3. Bake at 325°F for 75 to 85 minutes or until toothpick inserted near center comes out clean. Cool on cooling rack 20 minutes. Invert onto serving dish. Cool completely.

4. For glaze, combine 1 cup chocolate chips, ¹/₄ cup shortening and corn syrup in top part of double boiler over hot, not boiling, water. Stir until just melted and smooth. Cool slightly. (Or place mixture in microwave-safe bowl. Microwave at 50% (Medium) power for 1 minute and 15 seconds. Stir. Repeat at 15-second intervals, if necessary, until just melted and smooth. Cool slightly.) Spoon glaze over cake. Let stand until glaze is firm. *Makes 1 (10-inch) tube cake*

take-me-to-a-picnic cake

1 cup water
1 cup (2 sticks) butter or margarine
$^{1}/_{2}$ cup HERSHEY'S Cocoa
2 cups sugar
1$^{3}/_{4}$ cups all-purpose flour
1 teaspoon baking soda
$^{1}/_{2}$ teaspoon salt
3 eggs
$^{3}/_{4}$ cup dairy sour cream
Peanut Butter Chip Frosting (recipe follows)
Chocolate Garnish (optional, recipe follows)

1. Heat oven to 350°F. Grease and flour 15$^{1}/_{2}$×10$^{1}/_{2}$×1-inch jelly-roll pan.

2. Combine water, butter and cocoa in medium saucepan. Cook over medium heat, stirring occasionally, until mixture boils. Boil 1 minute. Remove from heat. Stir together sugar, flour, baking soda and salt in large bowl. Add eggs and sour cream; beat until blended. Add cocoa mixture; beat just until blended. Pour into prepared pan.

3. Bake 25 to 30 minutes or until wooden pick inserted in center comes out clean. Cool on wire rack. Prepare Peanut Butter Chip Frosting. Spread over cake. Prepare Chocolate Garnish; drizzle over top, if desired. *Makes about 20 servings*

peanut butter chip frosting: Combine $^{1}/_{3}$ cup butter or margarine, $^{1}/_{3}$ cup milk and 1$^{2}/_{3}$ cups (10-ounce package) REESE'S® Peanut Butter Chips in medium saucepan. Cook over low heat, stirring constantly, until chips are melted and mixture is smooth. Remove from heat; stir in 1 teaspoon vanilla extract. Place 1 cup powdered sugar in medium bowl. Gradually add chip mixture; beat well. Makes about 2 cups frosting.

chocolate garnish: Place $^{1}/_{2}$ cup HERSHEY'S Semi-Sweet Chocolate Chips and 1 teaspoon shortening (not butter, margarine, spread or oil) in small microwave-safe bowl. Microwave at HIGH (100%) 1 minute; stir until chips are melted and mixture is smooth.

Prep Time: 30 minutes
Bake Time: 25 minutes
Cool Time: 1 hour

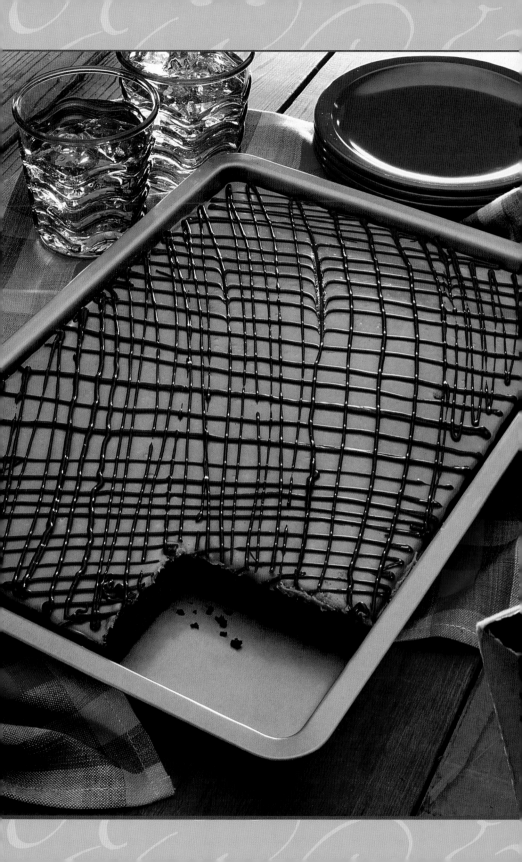

rich chocolate cake with creamy peanut butter milk chocolate frosting

Cake

>   2 cups all-purpose flour
>   1³/₄ cups granulated sugar
>   ²/₃ cup NESTLÉ® TOLL HOUSE® Baking Cocoa
>   1¹/₂ teaspoons baking powder
>   1¹/₂ teaspoons baking soda
>   ¹/₂ teaspoon salt
>   1 cup milk
>   1 cup water
>   ¹/₂ cup vegetable oil
>   2 large eggs
>   2 teaspoons vanilla extract
>   1²/₃ cups (11-ounce package) NESTLÉ® TOLL HOUSE®
>   Peanut Butter & Milk Chocolate Morsels, *divided*

Creamy Peanut Butter Milk Chocolate Frosting

>   1 package (8 ounces) cream cheese, softened
>   1 teaspoon vanilla extract
>   ¹/₈ teaspoon salt
>   3 cups powdered sugar

Garnish

>   1 bar (2 ounces *total*) NESTLÉ® TOLL HOUSE® Semi-Sweet
>   Chocolate Baking Bar, made into curls (see Tip)

For Cake

PREHEAT oven to 350°F. Grease and flour two 9-inch-round cake pans.

COMBINE flour, granulated sugar, cocoa, baking powder, baking soda and salt in large mixer bowl. Add milk, water, vegetable oil, eggs and vanilla extract; blend until moistened. Beat for 2 minutes (batter will be thin). Pour into prepared pans. Sprinkle ¹/₃ *cup* morsels over each cake layer.

BAKE for 25 to 30 minutes or until wooden pick inserted in center comes out clean. Cool in pans on wire racks for 10 minutes; remove to wire racks to cool completely. Frost with Creamy Peanut Butter Milk Chocolate Frosting between layers and on top and side of cake. Garnish with chocolate curls before serving.

continued on page 106

rich chocolate cake with creamy peanut butter milk chocolate frosting, continued

For Creamy Peanut Butter Milk Chocolate Frosting

MICROWAVE *remaining* morsels in small, uncovered, microwave-safe bowl on MEDIUM-HIGH (70%) power for 1 minute. STIR. Morsels may retain some of their original shape. If necessary, microwave at additional 10- to 15-second intervals, stirring just until morsels are melted. Beat cream cheese, melted morsels, vanilla extract and salt in small mixer bowl until light and fluffy. Gradually beat in powdered sugar. *Makes 10 to 12 servings*

tip: To make chocolate curls, carefully draw a vegetable peeler across a bar of NESTLÉ® TOLL HOUSE® Semi-Sweet Chocolate. Vary the width of your curls by using different sides of the chocolate bar.

slow cooker chocolate pudding cake

> 1 package (6-serving size) instant chocolate pudding and
>   pie filling mix
> 3 cups milk
> 1 package (about 18 ounces) chocolate fudge cake mix
>   plus ingredients to prepare mix
>   Whipped topping or ice cream (optional)

1. Spray 4-quart slow cooker with nonstick cooking spray. Place pudding mix in slow cooker. Whisk in milk.

2. Prepare cake mix according to package directions. Carefully pour cake mix into slow cooker. *Do not stir.* Cover; cook on HIGH 2½ hours or until cake is set.

3. Serve warm with whipped topping or ice cream, if desired.

Makes about 16 servings

mediterranean chocolate cake

Cake

- ³/₄ cup all-purpose flour
- ¹/₂ cup unsweetened cocoa powder
- ¹/₄ teaspoon baking soda
- ¹/₄ teaspoon ground cinnamon
- 4 large eggs
- ¹/₄ teaspoon salt
- 1 cup granulated sugar
- 2 teaspoons finely grated lemon peel
- ²/₃ cup FILIPPO BERIO® Olive Oil

Glaze

- 2 tablespoons water
- 1 cup powdered sugar
- ¹/₄ cup unsweetened cocoa powder
- 1 tablespoon FILIPPO BERIO® Olive Oil
- Pinch salt

For Cake, preheat oven to 350°F. Grease 9-inch round cake pan or 9-inch springform pan with olive oil. Line bottom of pan with parchment paper or waxed paper.

In small bowl, combine flour, cocoa, baking soda and cinnamon.

In large bowl, whisk together eggs and salt until blended. Slowly whisk in granulated sugar and lemon peel until combined. Sift flour mixture over egg mixture; fold in with rubber spatula until blended. Fold in olive oil, 2 tablespoons at a time, until well blended. Pour into prepared pan.

Bake 30 minutes or until cake springs back when pressed lightly in center. Cool on wire rack 10 minutes. Loosen cake from pan with knife or spatula. Invert onto wire rack; remove paper. Invert again; cool completely. Place cake on serving plate.

Meanwhile, for Glaze, in small saucepan, combine water and powdered sugar until smooth. Sift cocoa over sugar mixture; blend well. Stir in olive oil and salt. Warm glaze over low heat, stirring constantly, until just warm to the touch. Drizzle glaze over top of cake. Allow to set 10 minutes before serving.   *Makes 8 to 10 servings*

note: Cake may be prepared in advance and refrigerated or frozen. Thaw cake, loosely covered, at room temperature before adding glaze.

1 *unbaked* 9-inch (4-cup volume) deep-dish pie shell*
2 large eggs
½ cup all-purpose flour
½ cup granulated sugar
½ cup packed brown sugar
¾ cup (1½ sticks) butter, softened
1 cup (6 ounces) NESTLÉ® TOLL HOUSE® Semi-Sweet
    Chocolate Morsels
1 cup chopped nuts
    Sweetened whipped cream or ice cream (optional)

If using frozen pie shell, use deep-dish style, thawed completely. Bake on baking sheet; increase baking time slightly.

PREHEAT oven to 325°F.

BEAT eggs in large mixer bowl on high speed until foamy. Beat in flour, granulated sugar and brown sugar. Beat in butter. Stir in morsels and nuts. Spoon into pie shell.

BAKE for 55 to 60 minutes or until knife inserted halfway between outside edge and center comes out clean. Cool on wire rack. Serve warm with whipped cream.   *Makes 8 servings*

hot chocolate soufflé

³/₄ cup HERSHEY'S Cocoa
1 cup sugar, divided
¹/₂ cup all-purpose flour
¹/₄ teaspoon salt
2 cups milk
6 egg yolks, well beaten
2 tablespoons butter or margarine
1 teaspoon vanilla extract
8 egg whites
¹/₄ teaspoon cream of tartar
Sweetened whipped cream

1. Adjust oven rack to lowest position. Heat oven to 350°F. Lightly butter 2¹/₂-quart soufflé dish; sprinkle with sugar. For collar, cut a length of heavy-duty aluminum foil to fit around soufflé dish; fold in thirds lengthwise. Lightly butter one side of foil. Attach foil, buttered side in, around outside of dish, allowing foil to extend at least 2 inches above dish. Secure foil with tape or string.

2. Stir together cocoa, ³/₄ cup sugar, flour and salt in large saucepan; gradually stir in milk. Cook over medium heat, stirring constantly with wire whisk, until mixture boils; remove from heat. Gradually stir small amount of chocolate mixture into beaten egg yolks; blend well. Add egg mixture to chocolate mixture in pan, blending well. Cook and stir 1 minute. Add butter and vanilla, stirring until blended. Set aside; cool 20 minutes.

3. Beat egg whites with cream of tartar in large bowl until soft peaks form; gradually add remaining ¹/₄ cup sugar, beating until stiff peaks form. Gently fold about one-third of beaten egg white mixture into chocolate mixture. Lightly fold chocolate mixture, half at a time, into remaining beaten egg white mixture just until blended; do not overfold.

4. Gently pour mixture into prepared dish; smooth top with spatula. Gently place dish in larger baking pan; pour hot water into larger pan to depth of 1 inch.

5. Bake 65 to 70 minutes or until puffed and set. Remove soufflé dish from water. Carefully remove foil. Serve immediately with sweetened whipped cream. *Makes 8 to 10 servings*

brownie baked alaskas

2 purchased brownies (2½ inches square)
2 scoops fudge swirl ice cream or favorite flavor
⅓ cup semisweet chocolate chips
2 tablespoons light corn syrup or milk
2 egg whites
¼ cup sugar

1. Preheat oven to 500°F. Place brownies on small cookie sheet; top each with scoop of ice cream and place in freezer.

2. Melt chocolate chips in small saucepan over low heat. Stir in corn syrup; set aside and keep warm.

3. Beat egg whites to soft peaks in small bowl. Gradually beat in sugar; continue beating until stiff peaks form. Spread egg white mixture over ice cream and brownies with small spatula (ice cream and brownies should be completely covered with egg white mixture).

4. Bake 2 to 3 minutes or until meringue is golden. Spread chocolate sauce on serving plates; place baked Alaskas over sauce.

Makes 2 servings

Corn syrup is a thick, sweet and highly refined liquid made by treating cornstarch with acids and enzymes that cause it to liquefy. It comes in two varieties: Light corn syrup has been clarified and is clear and almost flavorless. Dark corn syrup has caramel flavoring and color added and has a stronger, molasses flavor. They can be used interchangeably unless a recipe directs otherwise.

chocolate fudge pie

Crust

1 unbaked Classic Crisco® Single Crust (page 116)

Filling

¼ CRISCO® Stick or ¼ cup CRISCO® all-vegetable shortening
1 bar (4 ounces) sweet baking chocolate
1 can (14 ounces) sweetened condensed milk
½ cup all-purpose flour
2 eggs, beaten
1 teaspoon vanilla
¼ teaspoon salt
1 cup flake coconut
1 cup chopped pecans

Garnish

Unsweetened whipped cream or ice cream

1. For crust, prepare as directed. Do not bake. Heat oven to 350°F. Place wire rack on countertop for cooling pie.

2. For filling, melt ¼ cup shortening and chocolate in heavy saucepan over low heat. Remove from heat. Stir in sweetened condensed milk, flour, eggs, vanilla and salt; mix well. Stir in coconut and nuts. Pour into unbaked pie crust.

3. Bake at 350°F for 40 minutes or until toothpick inserted into center comes out clean. Cool completely on cooling rack.

4. Serve with unsweetened whipped cream or ice cream, if desired. Refrigerate leftover pie.   *Makes 1 (9-inch) pie (8 servings)*

Prep Time: about 30 minutes
Bake Time: about 40 minutes

classic crisco® single crust

1⅓ cups all-purpose flour
½ teaspoon salt
½ CRISCO® Stick or ½ cup CRISCO® Shortening
3 tablespoons cold water

1. Spoon flour into measuring cup and level. Combine flour and salt in medium bowl.

2. Cut in ½ cup shortening using pastry blender or 2 knives until all flour is blended to form pea-size chunks.

3. Sprinkle with water, 1 tablespoon at a time. Toss lightly with fork until dough forms a ball.

4. Press dough between hands to form 5- to 6-inch "pancake." Flour rolling surface and rolling pin lightly. Roll dough into circle. Trim 1 inch larger than upside-down pie plate. Loosen dough carefully.

5. Fold dough into quarters. Unfold and press into pie plate. Fold edge under. Flute. *Makes 8- to 9-inch single crust*

When making a pie crust, add just enough water so that the mixture holds together with slight pressure and can be gathered into a ball. Handle the dough quickly and lightly, as a tough pie crust is often the result of too much flour worked into the dough and overhandling it.

chocolate nut apple strudel

1 sheet ($^1/_2$ of $17^1/_2$-ounce package) frozen puff pastry
1 cup finely shredded peeled apple
$^3/_4$ cup ground pecans
$^1/_2$ cup vanilla wafer crumbs (about 15 wafers)
$^1/_2$ cup HERSHEY'S Cocoa or HERSHEY'S Dutch Processed Cocoa
$^1/_3$ cup sugar
$^1/_4$ cup ($^1/_2$ stick) butter or margarine, melted
2 eggs, divided
$^1/_2$ teaspoon vanilla extract
2 teaspoons water
   Powdered Sugar Drizzle (recipe follows)
   Chocolate Chip Drizzle (recipe follows)

1. Thaw puff pastry according to package directions. Heat oven to 425°F. Sprinkle cookie sheet with cold water.

2. Stir together apple, pecans, crumbs and cocoa in medium bowl. Combine sugar, butter, 1 egg and vanilla in small bowl. Add to apple mixture; blend well.

3. Roll out pastry on lightly floured surface with floured rolling pin to 12×10-inch rectangle. Spoon apple mixture lengthwise down center of pastry. Lightly beat remaining 1 egg and water. Fold one side of pastry over apple mixture; brush long edge with egg mixture. Brush long edge of remaining side of pastry with egg mixture. Fold over filling; press edges together to seal. Place, seam side down, on prepared cookie sheet. Brush with remaining egg mixture.

4. Bake 20 to 25 minutes or until golden brown. Cool about 20 minutes. Prepare Powdered Sugar Drizzle and Chocolate Chip Drizzle; drizzle over warm strudel.   *Makes 10 to 12 servings*

powdered sugar drizzle: Stir together $^3/_4$ cup powdered sugar and $1^1/_2$ teaspoons milk in small bowl until smooth and of desired consistency. Add additional milk, $^1/_2$ teaspoon at a time, if needed.

chocolate chip drizzle: In small microwave-safe bowl, place $^1/_2$ cup HERSHEY'S Semi-Sweet Chocolate Chips and $1^1/_2$ teaspoons shortening (do *not* use butter, margarine or oil). Microwave at HIGH (100%) 30 seconds; stir. If necessary, microwave at HIGH an additional 15 seconds at a time, stirring after each heating, just until chips are melted when stirred.

cappuccino bon bons

1 (21-ounce) package DUNCAN HINES® Family-Style
  Chewy Fudge Brownie Mix
2 eggs
⅓ cup water
⅓ cup vegetable oil
1½ tablespoons instant coffee
1 teaspoon ground cinnamon
  Whipped topping
  Cinnamon

1. Preheat oven to 350°F. Place 2-inch foil cupcake liners on cookie sheet.

2. Combine brownie mix, eggs, water, oil, instant coffee and cinnamon. Stir with spoon until well blended, about 50 strokes. Fill each cupcake liner with 1 measuring tablespoon batter. Bake 12 to 15 minutes or until wooden toothpick inserted in center comes out clean. Cool completely. Garnish with whipped topping and a dash of cinnamon. Refrigerate until ready to serve.

Makes about 40 bon bons

tip: To make larger bon bons, use twelve 2½-inch foil cupcake liners and fill with ¼ cup batter. Bake 28 to 30 minutes.

decadent brownie pie

1 (9-inch) unbaked pastry shell
1 cup (6 ounces) semi-sweet chocolate chips
¼ cup (½ stick) butter or margarine
1 (14-ounce) can EAGLE BRAND® Sweetened Condensed Milk
    (NOT evaporated milk)
½ cup biscuit baking mix
2 eggs
1 teaspoon vanilla extract
1 cup chopped nuts
  Vanilla ice cream

1. Preheat oven to 375°F. Bake pastry shell 10 minutes; remove from oven. Reduce oven temperature to 325°F.

2. In small saucepan over low heat, melt chips with butter.

3. In large mixing bowl, beat chocolate mixture with Eagle Brand, biscuit mix, eggs and vanilla until smooth. Add nuts. Pour into baked pastry shell.

4. Bake 35 to 40 minutes or until center is set. Serve warm or at room temperature with ice cream. Refrigerate leftovers.

Makes 1 (9-inch) pie

Prep Time: 25 minutes
Bake Time: 45 to 50 minutes

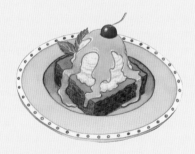

mini cocoa cupcake kabobs

1 cup sugar
1 cup all-purpose flour
$^1/_3$ cup HERSHEY'S Cocoa
$^3/_4$ teaspoon baking powder
$^3/_4$ teaspoon baking soda
$^1/_2$ teaspoon salt
1 egg
$^1/_2$ cup milk
$^1/_4$ cup vegetable oil
1 teaspoon vanilla extract
$^1/_2$ cup boiling water
    Lickety-Split Cocoa Frosting (recipe follows)
    Jelly beans or sugar nonpareils and/or decorating frosting
    Marshmallows
    Strawberries
    Wooden or metal skewers

1. Heat oven to 350°F. Spray small muffin cups ($1^3/_4$ inches in diameter) with vegetable cooking spray.

2. Stir together sugar, flour, cocoa, baking powder, baking soda and salt in medium bowl. Add egg, milk, oil and vanilla; beat on medium speed of mixer 2 minutes. Stir in boiling water (batter will be thin). Fill muffin cups about $^2/_3$ full with batter.

3. Bake 10 minutes or until wooden pick inserted in center comes out clean. Cool slightly; remove from pans to wire racks. Cool completely. Frost with Lickety-Split Cocoa Frosting. Garnish with jelly beans, nonpareils and/or white frosting piped onto cupcake. Alternate cupcakes, marshmallows and strawberries on skewers.

Makes about 4 dozen cupcakes

lickety-split cocoa frosting: Beat 3 tablespoons softened butter or margarine in small bowl until creamy. Add $1^1/_4$ cups powdered sugar, $^1/_4$ cup HERSHEY'S Cocoa, 2 to 3 tablespoons milk and $^1/_2$ teaspoon vanilla extract until smooth and of desired consistency. Makes about 1 cup frosting.

note: Number of kabobs will be determined by length of skewer used and number of cupcakes, marshmallows and strawberries placed on each skewer.

chocolate cinnamon bread pudding

   4 cups soft white bread cubes (5 slices)
 ½ cup chopped nuts
   3 eggs
 ¼ cup unsweetened cocoa
   2 teaspoons vanilla extract
   1 teaspoon ground cinnamon
 ½ teaspoon salt
2¾ cups water
   1 (14-ounce) can EAGLE BRAND® Sweetened Condensed Milk
      (NOT evaporated milk)
   2 tablespoons butter or margarine, melted
      Cinnamon Cream Sauce (recipe follows)

1. Preheat oven to 350°F. Place bread cubes and nuts in buttered
9-inch square baking pan. In large mixing bowl, beat eggs, cocoa,
vanilla, cinnamon and salt. Add water, Eagle Brand and butter;
mix well. Pour evenly over bread, moistening completely.

2. Bake 40 to 45 minutes or until knife inserted in center comes out
clean. Cool slightly. Serve warm topped with Cinnamon Cream Sauce.
Refrigerate leftovers.   *Makes 6 to 9 servings*

cinnamon cream sauce: In medium saucepan over medium-high
heat, combine 1 cup whipping cream, ⅔ cup firmly packed light
brown sugar, 1 teaspoon vanilla extract and ½ teaspoon ground
cinnamon. Bring to a boil; reduce heat and boil rapidly 6 to
8 minutes or until thickened, stirring occasionally. Serve warm.

chocolate cheesecake cupcakes

Cupcakes

2 cups (12-ounce package) NESTLÉ® TOLL HOUSE®
  Semi-Sweet Chocolate Morsels, *divided*
1½ cups all-purpose flour
1 teaspoon baking soda
½ teaspoon salt
½ cup granulated sugar
⅓ cup vegetable oil
1 large egg
1 teaspoon vanilla extract
1 cup water

Filling

2 packages (3 ounces *each*) cream cheese, softened
¼ cup granulated sugar
1 large egg
⅛ teaspoon salt

For Cupcakes

PREHEAT oven to 350°F. Grease or paper-line 16 muffin cups.

MICROWAVE ½ *cup* morsels in small, microwave-safe bowl on HIGH (100%) power for 45 seconds; stir. Microwave at additional 10- to 20-second intervals, stirring until smooth; cool to room temperature.

COMBINE flour, baking soda and salt in small bowl. Beat sugar, oil, egg and vanilla extract in large mixer bowl until blended. Beat in melted chocolate; gradually beat in flour mixture alternately with water (batter will be thin).

For Filling

BEAT cream cheese, sugar, egg and salt in small mixer bowl until creamy. Stir in *1 cup* morsels.

To Assemble

SPOON batter into prepared muffin cups, filling ½ full. Spoon filling by rounded tablespoon over batter. Spoon *remaining* batter over filling. Bake for 20 to 25 minutes or until wooden pick inserted in center comes out clean. While still hot, sprinkle with *remaining* ½ *cup* morsels. Let cool for 5 minutes or until morsels are shiny; spread to frost. Remove to wire racks to cool completely.

Makes 16 cupcakes

white chocolate bread pudding

5 cups (about 7 ounces) ³/₄-inch fresh Italian bread cubes
¹/₄ cup (¹/₂ stick) I CAN'T BELIEVE IT'S NOT BUTTER!® Spread, melted
6 ounces white chocolate, coarsely chopped
1 cup whipping or heavy cream
1 cup milk
3 eggs
¹/₂ cup sugar
1 tablespoon crème de cacao liqueur *or* 1 teaspoon vanilla extract
¹/₄ teaspoon salt

Grease 8-inch square baking dish; set aside.

In medium bowl, toss bread with melted I Can't Believe It's Not Butter!; arrange cubes in prepared dish and set aside.

In medium saucepan, melt chocolate with cream and milk over low heat, stirring occasionally. In large bowl with wire whisk, beat eggs, sugar, liqueur and salt. While beating slowly, drizzle in chocolate mixture. Pour over bread, pressing cubes down to coat evenly. Cover and refrigerate 2 hours.

Preheat oven to 350°F. Remove dish from refrigerator and remove cover. Press bread cubes down to coat with filling. Bake 30 minutes. Cover with aluminum foil and bake an additional 10 minutes or until knife inserted in center comes out clean and custard is set. Serve warm.

Makes 6 servings

chocolate for breakfast

blueberry white chip muffins

2 cups all-purpose flour
$^1/_2$ cup granulated sugar
$^1/_4$ cup packed brown sugar
$2^1/_2$ teaspoons baking powder
$^1/_2$ teaspoon salt
$^3/_4$ cup milk
1 large egg, lightly beaten
$^1/_4$ cup butter or margarine, melted
$^1/_2$ teaspoon grated lemon peel
2 cups (12-ounce package) NESTLÉ® TOLL HOUSE®
    Premier White Morsels, *divided*
$1^1/_2$ cups fresh or frozen blueberries
Streusel Topping (recipe follows)

PREHEAT oven to 375°F. Paper-line 18 muffin cups.

COMBINE flour, granulated sugar, brown sugar, baking powder and salt in large bowl. Stir in milk, egg, butter and lemon peel. Stir in *1$^1/_2$ cups* morsels and blueberries. Spoon into prepared muffin cups, filling almost full. Sprinkle with Streusel Topping.

BAKE for 22 to 25 minutes or until wooden pick inserted in center comes out clean. Cool in pans for 5 minutes; remove to wire racks to cool slightly.

PLACE *remaining* morsels in small, *heavy-duty* resealable plastic food storage bag. Microwave on MEDIUM-HIGH (70%) power for 30 seconds; knead. Microwave at additional 10- to 15-second intervals, kneading until smooth. Cut tiny corner from bag; squeeze to drizzle over muffins. Serve warm.   *Makes 18 muffins*

streusel topping: COMBINE $^1/_3$ cup granulated sugar, $^1/_4$ cup all-purpose flour and $^1/_4$ teaspoon ground cinnamon in small bowl. Cut in 3 tablespoons butter or margarine with pastry blender or two knives until mixture resembles coarse crumbs.

coconut chocolate chip loaf

1 package DUNCAN HINES® Bakery-Style Chocolate Chip
    Muffin Mix
1⅓ cups toasted flaked coconut (see Tip)
¾ cup water
1 egg
½ teaspoon vanilla extract
Confectioners' sugar for garnish (optional)

1. Preheat oven to 350°F. Grease and flour 9×5×3-inch loaf pan.

2. Empty muffin mix into medium bowl. Break up any lumps.
Add coconut, water, egg and vanilla extract. Stir until moistened,
about 50 strokes. Pour into prepared pan. Bake at 350°F for 45 to
50 minutes or until toothpick inserted in center comes out clean.
Cool in pan 15 minutes. Invert onto cooling rack. Turn right side
up. Cool completely. Dust with confectioners' sugar, if desired.

Makes 1 loaf (12 slices)

tip: Spread coconut evenly on baking sheet. Toast at 350°F for
5 minutes. Stir and toast 1 to 2 minutes longer or until light
golden brown.

orange streusel coffeecake

    Cocoa Streusel (recipe follows)
3/4 **cup (1 1/2 sticks) butter or margarine, softened**
1 **cup sugar**
3 **eggs**
1 **teaspoon vanilla extract**
1/2 **cup dairy sour cream**
3 **cups all-purpose flour**
2 **teaspoons baking powder**
1 **teaspoon baking soda**
1 **cup orange juice**
2 **teaspoons grated orange peel**
1/2 **cup orange marmalade or apple jelly**

1. Prepare Cocoa Streusel. Heat oven to 350°F. Generously grease 12-cup fluted tube pan.

2. Beat butter and sugar in large bowl until well blended. Add eggs and vanilla; beat well. Add sour cream; beat until blended. Stir together flour, baking powder and baking soda; add alternately with orange juice to butter mixture, beating until well blended. Stir in orange peel.

3. Spread marmalade in bottom of prepared pan; sprinkle half of streusel over marmalade. Pour half of batter into pan, spreading evenly. Sprinkle remaining streusel over batter; spread remaining batter evenly over streusel.

4. Bake about 1 hour or until toothpick inserted in center of cake comes out clean. Loosen cake from side of pan with metal spatula; immediately invert onto serving plate.   *Makes 12 servings*

cocoa streusel: Stir together 2/3 cup packed light brown sugar, 1/2 cup chopped walnuts, 1/4 cup HERSHEY'S Cocoa and 1/2 cup MOUNDS® Sweetened Coconut Flakes, if desired.

peanut butter mini muffins

$^1/_3$ cup creamy peanut butter
$^1/_4$ cup ($^1/_2$ stick) butter, softened
$^1/_4$ cup granulated sugar
$^1/_4$ cup firmly packed light brown sugar
 1 large egg
$^3/_4$ cup buttermilk
 3 tablespoons vegetable oil
$^3/_4$ teaspoon vanilla extract
$1^1/_2$ cups all-purpose flour
$^3/_4$ teaspoon baking powder
$^1/_2$ teaspoon baking soda
$^1/_2$ teaspoon salt
$1^1/_4$ cups "M&M's"® Milk Chocolate Mini Baking Bits, divided
   Chocolate Glaze (recipe follows)

Preheat oven to 350°F. Lightly grease 36 ($1^3/_4$-inch) mini muffin cups or line with paper or foil liners; set aside. In large bowl cream peanut butter, butter and sugars until light and fluffy; beat in egg. Beat in buttermilk, oil and vanilla. In medium bowl combine flour, baking powder, baking soda and salt; gradually blend into creamed mixture. Divide batter evenly among prepared muffin cups. Sprinkle batter evenly with $^3/_4$ cup "M&M's"® Milk Chocolate Mini Baking Bits. Bake 15 to 17 minutes or until toothpick inserted in centers comes out clean. Cool completely on wire racks. Prepare Chocolate Glaze. Place glaze in resealable plastic sandwich bag; seal bag. Cut tiny piece off one corner of bag (not more than $^1/_8$ inch). Drizzle glaze over muffins. Decorate with remaining $^1/_2$ cup "M&M's"® Milk Chocolate Mini Baking Bits; let glaze set. Store in tightly covered container.

Makes 3 dozen mini muffins

chocolate glaze: In top of double boiler over hot water melt 2 (1-ounce) squares semi-sweet chocolate and 1 tablespoon butter. Stir until smooth; let cool slightly.

petit pain au chocolate

1 package (17.25 ounces) frozen puff pastry sheets, thawed
1 cup (6 ounces) NESTLÉ® TOLL HOUSE® Milk Chocolate
    Morsels, *divided*
1 large egg, beaten
1 bar (2 ounces *total*) NESTLÉ® TOLL HOUSE® Semi-Sweet
    Chocolate Baking Bars, broken into pieces
2 tablespoons butter or margarine
1 cup powdered sugar
2 tablespoons hot water

PREHEAT oven to 350°F. Grease 2 baking sheets.

UNFOLD *1* pastry sheet on lightly floured surface. Roll out to make 10-inch square. Cut into 4 squares. Place *2 tablespoons* morsels in center of each square. Brush edges lightly with beaten egg and fold squares to form triangles. Press edges to seal. Place on prepared baking sheet about 2 inches apart. Repeat with *remaining* pastry sheet. Brush top of each pastry with beaten egg.

BAKE for 15 to 17 minutes or until puffed and golden. Cool on baking sheets for 2 minutes; remove to wire racks to cool completely.

MELT baking bar and butter in small, uncovered, microwave-safe bowl on HIGH (100%) power for 30 seconds. STIR. Bar may retain some of its original shape. If necessary, microwave at additional 10- to 15-second intervals, stirring just until bar is melted. Stir in sugar. Add water, stirring until icing is smooth, adding additional water, if necessary. Drizzle icing over pastries. *Makes 8 pastries*

Puff pastry is a rich but delicate and flaky multilayered dough. It is created by layering thin sheets of pastry dough with bits of butter, then rolling, folding and repeating the process 6 to 8 times, ultimately resulting in a pastry made of hundreds of layers of dough and butter. When baked, the moisture in the melting butter creates steam, causing the pastry to puff and separate into flaky layers.

chocolate chip coffeecake

    3 cups all-purpose flour, divided
    $^1/_3$ cup sugar
    2 envelopes FLEISCHMANN'S® RapidRise™ Yeast
    1 teaspoon salt
    $^1/_2$ cup milk
    $^1/_2$ cup water
    $^1/_2$ cup butter or margarine
    2 large eggs
    $^3/_4$ cup semi-sweet chocolate morsels
       Chocolate Nut Topping (recipe follows)

In large bowl, combine 1 cup flour, sugar, undissolved yeast and
salt. Heat milk, water and butter until very warm (120° to 130°F).
Gradually add to dry ingredients. Beat 2 minutes at medium speed
of electric mixer, scraping bowl occasionally. Add eggs and 1 cup
flour; beat 2 minutes at high speed, scraping bowl occasionally. Stir in
chocolate morsels and remaining flour to make a soft batter. Turn into
greased 13×9×2-inch baking pan. Cover; let rise in warm, draft-free
place until doubled in size, about 1 hour.

Bake at 400°F for 15 minutes; remove from oven and sprinkle
with Chocolate Nut Topping. Return to oven and bake additional
10 minutes or until done. Cool in pan for 10 minutes. Remove from
pan; cool on wire rack.   *Makes 1 cake*

chocolate nut topping: In medium bowl, cut $^1/_2$ cup butter into $^2/_3$ cup
all-purpose flour until crumbly. Stir in $^2/_3$ cup sugar, 2 teaspoons
ground cinnamon, 1 cup semi-sweet chocolate morsels and 1 cup
chopped pecans.

banana chocolate chip muffins

2 ripe, medium DOLE® Bananas
1 cup packed brown sugar
2 eggs
$^1\!/_2$ cup margarine, melted
1 teaspoon vanilla extract
$2^1\!/_4$ cups all-purpose flour
2 teaspoons baking powder
$^1\!/_2$ teaspoon ground cinnamon
$^1\!/_2$ teaspoon salt
1 cup chocolate chips
$^1\!/_2$ cup chopped walnuts

• Purée bananas in blender (1 cup). Beat bananas, sugar, eggs, margarine and vanilla in medium bowl until well blended.

• Combine flour, baking powder, cinnamon and salt in large bowl. Stir in chocolate chips and nuts. Make well in center of dry ingredients. Add banana mixture. Stir just until blended. Spoon into well greased $2^1\!/_2$-inch muffin pan cups.

• Bake at 350°F 25 to 30 minutes or until toothpick inserted in centers comes out clean. Cool slightly; remove from pan and place on wire rack.   *Makes 12 muffins*

Prep Time: 20 minutes
Bake Time: 30 minutes

lots o' chocolate bread

$^2/_3$ cup packed light brown sugar
$^1/_2$ cup (1 stick) butter, softened
  2 cups miniature semisweet chocolate chips, divided
  2 eggs
$2^1/_2$ cups all-purpose flour
$1^1/_2$ cups applesauce
$1^1/_2$ teaspoons vanilla
  1 teaspoon baking soda
  1 teaspoon baking powder
$^1/_2$ teaspoon salt
  1 tablespoon shortening (do not use butter, margarine,
     spread or oil)

1. Preheat oven to 350°F. Grease 5 ($5^1/_2 \times 3$-inch) mini loaf pans. Beat brown sugar and butter in large bowl with electric mixer until creamy. Melt 1 cup miniature chocolate chips; cool slightly and add to sugar mixture with eggs. Add flour, applesauce, vanilla, baking soda, baking powder and salt; beat until well blended. Stir in $^1/_2$ cup chocolate chips. Spoon batter into prepared pans; bake 35 to 40 minutes or until center cracks and is dry to the touch. Cool 10 minutes before removing from pans.

2. Place remaining $^1/_2$ cup chocolate chips and shortening in small microwavable bowl. Microwave at HIGH 1 minute; stir. If necessary, microwave at HIGH at additional 15-second intervals, stirring after each interval. Drizzle glaze over warm loaves. Cool completely.

Makes 5 mini loaves

cocoa nut bundles →

1 can (8 ounces) refrigerated quick crescent dinner rolls
2 tablespoons butter or margarine, softened
1 tablespoon granulated sugar
2 teaspoons HERSHEY'S Cocoa
$1/4$ cup chopped nuts
   Powdered sugar (optional)

1. Heat oven to 375°F. On ungreased cookie sheet, unroll dough and separate to form 8 triangles.

2. Combine butter, granulated sugar and cocoa in small bowl. Add nuts; mix thoroughly. Divide chocolate mixture evenly among the triangles, placing on wide end of triangle. Take dough on either side of mixture and pull up and over mixture, tucking ends under. Continue rolling dough toward the opposite point.

3. Bake 9 to 10 minutes or until golden brown. Sprinkle with powdered sugar; serve warm.

Makes 8 rolls

orange chocolate chip bread

$1/2$ cup nonfat milk
$1/2$ cup plain nonfat yogurt
$1/3$ cup sugar
$1/4$ cup orange juice
 1 egg, slightly beaten
 1 tablespoon freshly grated orange peel
 3 cups all-purpose biscuit baking mix
$1/2$ cup HERSHEY'S MINI CHIPS™ Semi-Sweet Chocolate Chips

1. Heat oven to 350°F. Grease 9×5×3-inch loaf pan or spray with vegetable cooking spray.

2. Stir together milk, yogurt, sugar, orange juice, egg and orange peel in large bowl; add baking mix. With spoon, beat until well blended, about 1 minute. Stir in small chocolate chips. Pour into prepared pan.

3. Bake 45 to 50 minutes or until wooden pick inserted in center comes out clean. Cool 10 minutes; remove from pan to wire rack. Cool completely before slicing. Garnish as desired. Wrap leftover bread in foil or plastic wrap. Store at room temperature or freeze for longer storage.

Makes 1 loaf (16 slices)

toll house® crumbcake

Topping

- ⅓ cup packed brown sugar
- 1 tablespoon all-purpose flour
- 2 tablespoons butter or margarine, softened
- ½ cup chopped nuts
- 2 cups (12-ounce package) NESTLÉ® TOLL HOUSE® Semi-Sweet Chocolate Mini Morsels, *divided*

Cake

- 1¾ cups all-purpose flour
- 1 teaspoon baking powder
- 1 teaspoon baking soda
- ¼ teaspoon salt
- ¾ cup granulated sugar
- ½ cup (1 stick) butter or margarine, softened
- 1 teaspoon vanilla extract
- 3 large eggs
- 1 cup sour cream

PREHEAT oven to 350°F. Grease 13×9-inch baking pan.

For Topping

COMBINE brown sugar, flour and butter in small bowl with pastry blender or two knives until crumbly. Stir in nuts and *½ cup* morsels.

For Cake

COMBINE flour, baking powder, baking soda and salt in small bowl. Beat granulated sugar, butter and vanilla extract in large mixer bowl until creamy. Add eggs, one at a time, beating well after each addition. Gradually add flour mixture alternately with sour cream. Fold in *remaining* morsels. Spread into prepared baking pan; sprinkle with topping.

BAKE for 25 to 35 minutes or until wooden pick inserted in center comes out clean. Cool in pan on wire rack.   *Makes 12 servings*

chocolate popovers

$\frac{3}{4}$ cup plus 2 tablespoons all-purpose flour
$\frac{1}{4}$ cup granulated sugar
  2 tablespoons unsweetened cocoa powder
$\frac{1}{4}$ teaspoon salt
  4 eggs
  1 cup milk
  2 tablespoons butter, melted
$\frac{1}{2}$ teaspoon vanilla
  Powdered sugar

1. Position rack in lower third of oven. Preheat oven to 375°F. Grease 6-cup popover pan or 6 (6-ounce) custard cups. Set custard cups in jelly-roll pan for easier handling.

2. Sift flour, granulated sugar, cocoa and salt into medium bowl; set aside. Beat eggs at low speed of electric mixer 1 minute. Beat in milk, butter and vanilla. Beat in flour mixture until smooth. Pour batter into prepared pan. Bake 50 minutes.

3. Place waxed paper under wire rack. Immediately remove popovers to wire rack. Place powdered sugar in fine-mesh sieve. Generously sprinkle powdered sugar over popovers. Serve immediately.

Makes 6 popovers

fudgey peanut butter chip muffins

^{1}/$_2$ cup applesauce
^{1}/$_2$ cup quick-cooking rolled oats
^{1}/$_4$ cup (^{1}/$_2$ stick) butter or margarine, softened
^{1}/$_2$ cup granulated sugar
^{1}/$_2$ cup packed light brown sugar
  1 egg
^{1}/$_2$ teaspoon vanilla extract
^{3}/$_4$ cup all-purpose flour
^{1}/$_4$ cup HERSHEY'S Dutch Processed Cocoa or HERSHEY'S Cocoa
^{1}/$_2$ teaspoon baking soda
^{1}/$_4$ teaspoon ground cinnamon (optional)
  1 cup REESE'S® Peanut Butter Chips
    Powdered sugar (optional)

1. Heat oven to 350°F. Line muffin cups (2^1/$_2$ inches in diameter) with paper bake cups.

2. Stir together applesauce and oats in small bowl; set aside. Beat butter, granulated sugar, brown sugar, egg and vanilla in large bowl until well blended. Add applesauce mixture; blend well. Stir together flour, cocoa, baking soda and cinnamon, if desired. Add to butter mixture, blending well. Stir in peanut butter chips. Fill muffin cups ^{3}/$_4$ full with batter.

3. Bake 22 to 26 minutes or until wooden pick inserted in center comes out almost clean. Cool slightly in pan on wire rack. Sprinkle muffin tops with powdered sugar, if desired. Serve warm.

Makes 12 to 15 muffins

fudgey chocolate chip muffins: Omit Peanut Butter Chips. Add 1 cup HERSHEY'S Semi-Sweet Chocolate Chips.

double chocolate zucchini muffins

2⅓ cups all-purpose flour
1¼ cups sugar
⅓ cup unsweetened cocoa powder
2 teaspoons baking powder
1½ teaspoons ground cinnamon
1 teaspoon baking soda
½ teaspoon salt
1 cup sour cream
½ cup vegetable oil
2 eggs, beaten
¼ cup milk
1 cup milk chocolate chips
1 cup shredded zucchini

1. Preheat oven to 400°F. Grease 12 (3½-inch) large muffin cups.

2. Combine flour, sugar, cocoa, baking powder, cinnamon, baking soda and salt in large bowl. Combine sour cream, oil, eggs and milk in small bowl until blended; stir into flour mixture just until moistened. Fold in chips and zucchini. Spoon into prepared muffin cups, filling ½ full.

3. Bake 25 to 30 minutes until wooden toothpick inserted into centers comes out clean. Cool in pan on wire rack 5 minutes. Remove from pan. Cool on wire rack. Store tightly covered at room temperature.

Makes 12 jumbo muffins

donna's heavenly orange chip scones

4 cups all-purpose flour
1 cup granulated sugar
4 teaspoons baking powder
$\frac{1}{2}$ teaspoon baking soda
$\frac{1}{2}$ teaspoon salt
1 cup (6 ounces) NESTLÉ® TOLL HOUSE® Semi-Sweet
    Chocolate Mini Morsels
1 cup golden raisins
1 tablespoon grated orange peel
1 cup (2 sticks) unsalted butter, cut into pieces and softened
1 cup buttermilk
3 large eggs, *divided*
1 teaspoon orange extract
1 tablespoon milk
    Icing (recipe follows)

PREHEAT oven to 350°F. Lightly grease baking sheets.

COMBINE flour, granulated sugar, baking powder, baking soda and salt in large bowl. Add morsels, raisins and orange peel; mix well. Cut in butter with pastry blender or two knives until mixture resembles coarse crumbs. Combine buttermilk, *2 eggs* and orange extract in small bowl. Pour buttermilk mixture into flour mixture; mix just until a sticky dough is formed. Do not overmix. Drop by $\frac{1}{4}$ cupfuls onto prepared baking sheets. Combine *remaining* egg and milk in small bowl. Brush egg mixture over top of dough.

BAKE for 18 to 22 minutes or until wooden pick inserted in center comes out clean. For best results, bake one baking sheet at a time. Cool on wire racks for 10 minutes. Drizzle scones with icing. Serve warm.   *Makes 2 dozen scones*

icing: **COMBINE** 2 cups powdered sugar, $\frac{1}{4}$ cup orange juice, 1 tablespoon grated orange peel and 1 teaspoon orange extract in medium bowl. Mix until smooth.

white chocolate chunk muffins

2½ cups all-purpose flour
1 cup packed brown sugar
⅓ cup unsweetened cocoa powder
2 teaspoons baking soda
½ teaspoon salt
1⅓ cups buttermilk
6 tablespoons butter, melted
2 eggs, beaten
1½ teaspoons vanilla
1½ cups chopped white chocolate

1. Preheat oven to 400°F. Grease 12 (3½-inch) large muffin cups; set aside.

2. Combine flour, sugar, cocoa, baking soda and salt in large bowl. Combine buttermilk, butter, eggs and vanilla in small bowl until blended. Stir into flour mixture just until moistened. Fold in white chocolate. Spoon into prepared muffin cups, filling half full.

3. Bake 25 to 30 minutes or until toothpick inserted into centers comes out clean. Cool in pan on wire rack 5 minutes. Remove from pan. Cool on wire rack 10 minutes. Serve warm or cool completely.

Makes 12 jumbo muffins

Fresh milk can be soured and used as a substitute for buttermilk. If a recipe calls for 1 cup of buttermilk, place 1 tablespoon lemon juice or distilled white vinegar in a measuring cup and add enough milk to measure 1 cup. Stir and let the mixture stand at room temperature for 5 minutes. (For the 1⅓ cups buttermilk in this recipe, use 4 teaspoons lemon juice or vinegar plus enough milk to measure 1⅓ cups.)

chocolate streusel pecan muffins

Topping

- ¼ cup all-purpose flour
- ¼ cup packed brown sugar
- ¼ teaspoon ground cinnamon
- 2 tablespoons butter, melted
- ¼ cup chopped pecans

Muffins

- 1¾ cups (11.5-ounce package) NESTLÉ® TOLL HOUSE® Milk Chocolate Morsels, *divided*
- ⅓ cup milk
- 3 tablespoons butter
- 1 cup all-purpose flour
- 2 tablespoons granulated sugar
- 2 teaspoons baking powder
- ¼ teaspoon ground cinnamon
- ¾ cup chopped pecans
- 1 large egg
- ½ teaspoon vanilla extract

For Topping

COMBINE flour, brown sugar, cinnamon and butter in small bowl with fork until mixture resembles coarse crumbs. Stir in nuts.

For Muffins

PREHEAT oven to 375°F. Grease or paper-line 12 muffin cups.

COMBINE *1 cup* morsels, milk and butter over hot (not boiling) water. Stir until morsels are melted and mixture is smooth.

COMBINE flour, granulated sugar, baking powder, cinnamon, pecans and *remaining* morsels in large bowl.

COMBINE egg, vanilla extract and melted morsel mixture in small bowl; stir into flour mixture just until moistened. Spoon into prepared muffin cups, filling ⅔ full. Sprinkle with topping.

BAKE for 20 to 25 minutes. Cool in pan for 5 minutes; remove to wire rack to cool completely. *Makes 12 muffins*

acknowledgments

*The publisher would like to thank the companies and organizations
listed below for the use of their recipes and photographs
in this publication.*

ConAgra Foods®

Dole Food Company, Inc.

Domino® Foods, Inc.

Duncan Hines® and Moist Deluxe® are registered trademarks
of Aurora Foods Inc.

Eagle Brand®

Egg Beaters®

Filippo Berio® Olive Oil

Fleischmann's® Yeast

Hershey Foods Corporation

Kahlúa® Liqueur

© Mars, Incorporated 2004

McIlhenny Company (TABASCO® brand Pepper Sauce)

National Honey Board

Nestlé USA

The Quaker® Oatmeal Kitchens

Reckitt Benckiser Inc.

The J.M. Smucker Company

Texas Peanut Producers Board

Unilever Bestfoods North America

index

METRIC CONVERSION CHART

VOLUME MEASUREMENTS (dry)

1/8 teaspoon = 0.5 mL
1/4 teaspoon = 1 mL
1/2 teaspoon = 2 mL
3/4 teaspoon = 4 mL
1 teaspoon = 5 mL
1 tablespoon = 15 mL
2 tablespoons = 30 mL
1/4 cup = 60 mL
1/3 cup = 75 mL
1/2 cup = 125 mL
2/3 cup = 150 mL
3/4 cup = 175 mL
1 cup = 250 mL
2 cups = 1 pint = 500 mL
3 cups = 750 mL
4 cups = 1 quart = 1 L

VOLUME MEASUREMENTS (fluid)

1 fluid ounce (2 tablespoons) = 30 mL
4 fluid ounces (1/2 cup) = 125 mL
8 fluid ounces (1 cup) = 250 mL
12 fluid ounces (1 1/2 cups) = 375 mL
16 fluid ounces (2 cups) = 500 mL

WEIGHTS (mass)

1/2 ounce = 15 g
1 ounce = 30 g
3 ounces = 90 g
4 ounces = 120 g
8 ounces = 225 g
10 ounces = 285 g
12 ounces = 360 g
16 ounces = 1 pound = 450 g

DIMENSIONS

1/16 inch = 2 mm
1/8 inch = 3 mm
1/4 inch = 6 mm
1/2 inch = 1.5 cm
3/4 inch = 2 cm
1 inch = 2.5 cm

OVEN TEMPERATURES

250°F = 120°C
275°F = 140°C
300°F = 150°C
325°F = 160°C
350°F = 180°C
375°F = 190°C
400°F = 200°C
425°F = 220°C
450°F = 230°C

BAKING PAN SIZES

Utensil	Size in Inches/Quarts	Metric Volume	Size in Centimeters
Baking or Cake Pan (square or rectangular)	8×8×2	2 L	20×20×5
	9×9×2	2.5 L	23×23×5
	12×8×2	3 L	30×20×5
	13×9×2	3.5 L	33×23×5
Loaf Pan	8×4×3	1.5 L	20×10×7
	9×5×3	2 L	23×13×7
Round Layer Cake Pan	8×1½	1.2 L	20×4
	9×1½	1.5 L	23×4
Pie Plate	8×1¼	750 mL	20×3
	9×1¼	1 L	23×3
Baking Dish or Casserole	1 quart	1 L	—
	1½ quart	1.5 L	—
	2 quart	2 L	—